D1320378

THE INTERPRETATION OF HISTORY

THE INTERPRETATION OF HISTORY

BY

Jacques Barzun

Hajo Holborn

Herbert Heaton

Dumas Malone

George La Piana

EDITED WITH AN INTRODUCTION BY

Joseph R. Strayer

NEW YORK

PETER SMITH

1950

Contents

INTRODUCTION

By JOSEPH R. STRAYER

Introduction

THE ordinary historian has always been somewhat embarrassed when asked to justify his devotion to his subject. Interest in history seems to him natural and inevitable; it no more needs explanation than the act of breathing. If he is completely honest with himself, he will wonder if his original decision to concentrate on the study of history was not due more to the fact that it gave him pleasure than to any profound conviction of its value and significance. When under attack, he may develop elaborate arguments to prove the social usefulness of his work, but these bursts of enthusiasm are apt to leave him with the uneasy feeling that he has yielded to the common human failing of inventing good reasons for doing what he would have done in any case. Nagging by scientists and social scientists may drive him to formulate laws of historical research, but the next day he will be wondering if he has not invented a complicated terminology to disguise a method which must be based more on instinct and common sense than on the principles of the physical sciences. History, at least in its final stages, is more of an art than a science, and historians, like artists, have seldom been able to describe their work in purely intellectual terms. In both cases there is a belief that a certain arrangement of carefully selected facts will illustrate some aspect of universal truth, and a feeling that this belief can never be fully justified by purely rational arguments.

This normal reluctance of historians to discuss the validity and significance of their work has been weakened in recent years by both external and internal criticism. Writers who are not historians have had no hesitation in explaining to the world just what history is and what it should do. Their ideas have often been helpful, since men viewing the subject from the outside may see its general characteristics and relations to other activities more clearly than those who are always burrowing deeper into the mountain of historical facts. At the same time, these appraisals by outsiders have led to such contradictory conclusions that working historians have been somewhat bewildered. Thus one school of critics tells them that they are so full of conscious and unconscious prejudices that they can never hope to tell the truth—if, indeed, there is such a thing as historical truth. Another group admits that they are truthful but damns them as cowards because they will not try to develop from their studies a few simple laws of human behavior which would explain the past, present and future of all societies. Historians are useless because they can never achieve certainty, and they are slackers because they refuse to draw blueprints for a brave, new world from their poor, fallible pseudo-knowledge. Other studies can show men the narrow road to salvation, but history mercly leads its devotees into a revolving squirrel cage of doubt and confusion.

Most historians feel reasonably sure that their discipline is neither as influential nor as contemptible as these critics would claim. History, they would say, may not be the neglected gateway to a new "science of society" or a new "religion of humanity" but it is more than "a pack of tricks we play on the dead." History at its best merely suggests; it cannot command. History at its worst distorts reality, but cannot escape from it entirely. But in reacting to these criticisms historians have been forced to reconsider their traditional beliefs, procedures and objectives. They have realized that the old view of history placed too much emphasis on individual values and not enough on social values. History must be more than an adornment for the cultivated gentleman, more than a pastime for the intellectually curious, more than a tower of refuge for the skeptic and the philosopher. It must be a guide to action, not an excuse for contemplation.

The essays included in this volume show how widely interest in the problems of the value and significance of history has spread. Here we have scholars who received their original training in France, Germany, England, Italy, and the United States all concerned with the question of the interpretation of history. As the title indicates, they have not tried to deal with all aspects of historiography—for which, indeed, there was scarcely space—but rather with "history as communication," to borrow Professor Barzun's admirable phrase. That is to say, how does, or how should, the historian proceed in his effort to make available to laymen the products of scholarly research, what results does he expect from this effort, how are these results modified by other interests and beliefs of his readers?

If we, in this volume, are dealing with the communication of history, we must first define what it is that we are seeking to communicate. What is history? The only possible answer is that history is the study of all past human activities. This is a broad and ambitious program—so broad that scholars in other fields accuse historians of invading their preserves, so ambitious that no single historian or group of historians can ever hope to fulfill it. Yet it is hard to see how history may be confined within narrower limits. All human activities are interrelated, and none is so trivial that it may not influence or illustrate others which seem more important. The tools men use or the food they eat may determine the chances for survival of a people; the games they play or the stories they read may establish the character of a nation. The conscientious historian may even wonder if he should not know something of the past of the earth and all that is therein. Changes in climate may have influenced men more than wars, and the migration of the herring from the Baltic to the North Sea may have been as important in the history of English commerce as the voyages of discovery.

At one time, the chief problem of the historian was to discover records of the past activities which he wished to investigate. Development of research techniques in history and allied subjects has almost solved this problem. Historians have learned that most human activity leaves some sort of trace behind it, and they have become more and more expert in learning where to look for these relics of the past. Available written records have been classified and catalogued, and students of history are giving an increasing amount of attention to other types of evidence. Written records are not the only, nor are they necessarily the best sources for gaining an understanding of the past. A scholar who tried to write the history of agriculture in the Roman and early medieval periods from written records alone would have little to say. He would soon find that he must study archeological relics which happen to illustrate methods of harnessing and using animals—fragments of ancient tools, votive offerings, children's toys, and art objects. He would learn that the earth itself has preserved traces of ancient field-systems and that photographs taken from an airplane will reveal primitive patterns of cultivation. There are few written records dealing with the early history of commerce, but hoards of coins or precious objects found in tombs make it possible to map out the great trade-routes of the ancient world. Even for more recent periods, written records must be supplemented by other evidence. The first signs of a distinctly American culture are found in houses and furniture rather than in written records or books, and the influence of new groups of immigrants may be more evident to a lover of regional cooking than to a student of government documents.

The discovery and classification of a great body of source materials has simplified one of the historian's problems and has tremendously complicated another. This problem, in its simplest terms, is to find a pattern in, or impose a pattern upon, a multitude of individual facts. There are always more facts available than any historian can master; he can deal with them only by arranging them in categories, and by generalizing from the classifications which he has made. Yet he knows that no one historical event is exactly like another, and that a single difference may be more significant than many resemblances. He must always wonder whether the pattern which he sees in history is really justified by the facts, and he is often troubled by the feeling that the more facts he knows the less clear the pattern becomes. To take an extreme example, it would be very difficult for anyone to assimilate, classify and reduce to general terms all the factual statements in a single issue of the *New York Times*. Yet the modern historian is supposed to accomplish this feat for the great files of newspapers which stretch back into the eighteenth century. And these are by no means the bulkiest or the most detailed records available to the historian. There are the records of the English courts, which run in an uninterrupted series for over seven centuries, and which are so voluminous that no historian has even attempted to analyze them. There are the records of bankers, merchants, and manufacturers, which become numerous in the fourteenth century and almost unmanageable in the modern period. Only by confining himself to brief chronological periods can the historian hope to deal with the mass of material which is available, and even then he has solved only half his problem. He has reduced the number of facts to manageable proportions, but he still must find the significance of the facts with which he deals. He must establish some principles for the interpretation of history; he must ask himself fundamental questions about the nature of his discipline.

What is the value of history to the individual and to society? Is it worth the time and effort which it requires? And, granting that history has certain values, how can these be best attained?

To answer these questions it is necessary to forget formal history for a moment and to consider the ideas and behavior of the ordinary man. If we do this, it is at once evident that man is essentially and incorrigibly historically-minded, and that this is one of the traits which separates him most clearly from the other animals. He can plan for the future only because he remembers the past; he can add to his knowledge only because he does not lose the memory of former experiences. Everyone, from the peasant to the scholar, tries to meet new situations by discovering familiar elements which make it possible to evoke analogies with the past. When, as sometimes happens, a man forgets his own personal history, he is useless to himself and society until he has recovered his past, or created a new past as a substitute for the old. The unfortunate individuals who cannot remember or cannot use their past experiences are considered feeble-minded and are treated as inferiors. In short, to twist Becker's famous phrase a little, every man must be his own historian if he is to be fully a man. What is true of individuals is also true of societies. No community can survive and no institution can function without constant reference to past experience. We are ruled by precedents fully as much as by laws, which is to say that we are ruled by collective memory of the past. It is the memory of common experiences which makes scattered individuals into a community, just as it is the memory of his own experiences which makes a child into a man. This memory of common experiences does not always reach the level of history, since a primitive people has little sense of chronology and is apt to stir all its past into a timeless brew of custom. But as soon as a community substitutes conscious decisions and rational choices for the automatic responses of custom it finds that its memories of the past must be kept distinct and arranged in some sort of order. Every deliberate modification of an existing type of activity must be based on a study of individual precedents. Every plan for the future is dependent on a pattern which has been found in the past.

Thus history is an essential part of civilized human life, and it is futile to argue whether we shall or shall not devote some attention to it. The real problem, as Professor Barzun points out in his lecture, is to improve the quality of the history which we use. History is a guide to life, but too often the indications which it gives are vague, incomplete, or actually misleading. The task of the professional historian is to remedy these defects as far as he can.

The difference between history which is a reliable guide and history which is not is more than the difference between accuracy and inaccuracy. The layman is apt to suppose that if each individual statement of fact in an historical work is correct the whole book is trustworthy. This belief involves a serious misunderstanding of the nature and function of historical writing. In most cases, the easiest, the most mechanical part of the historian's task is to establish the truth of individual facts. Even when his sources are inaccurate or incomplete he possesses recognized techniques for dealing with prejudiced authorities, for detecting forged and altered documents, for establishing a proper chronological sequence in a series of undated events. A properly trained historian is as careful as a scientist in his use of evidence, and his statements of fact have equal validity. In fact, we have rather better evidence for saying that the Battle of Jutland took place on May 30, 1916, than for saying that water is composed of two atoms of hydrogen and one of oxygen, since the first statement is based on the direct personal experience of thousands of men while the second is based only on inference.

But establishing the truth of an individual fact, or even the truth of a whole series of facts, is not history. If history is to be a guide to life it must deal with whole situations, not mere isolated facts; it must deal with causes and effects, not mere chronological sequences. It would be quite possible to write an account of the Battle of Jutland describing, with a high degree of accuracy, every movement of every ship which took part in the engagement, but such an account would not be a history of the battle, and no one would be very anxious to read it. What we want to know about Jutland is why the battle took place, why the Germans scored their initial successes, why the British failed to cut off the German retreat, what effect the battle had on the course of the war, how a modern naval battle differs from one in the past, and what modifications of accepted principles of strategy, tactics, and naval construction were suggested by the battle. These questions can be answered only by massing many facts together to give a general impression, and by linking these groups of facts to establish a sequence of causes and effects.

This massing and linking of facts is not only essential, if history is to have any value; it is also inevitable, since it is the way in which the human mind deals with any past experience. Essential and inevitable though it be, it is the point of greatest danger in all historical writing. It is obvious that facts can be massed in such a way as to produce a misleading impression, even though each individual fact may be true. Any judicial system may be made to appear obnoxious by dwelling only on cases in which there have been clear miscarriages of justice. Any foreign country may be rendered ridiculous or hateful by stressing certain aspects of its history. Individuals and communities may become convinced that the whole world is conspiring against them, if they remember only the occasions on which they have been treated unjustly.

Even more dangerous, because more apt to be the result of unconscious error, are the mistakes which can be made in trying to establish sequences of causes and effects.[1] The causes of any historical event are always

[1] Not being a systematic philosopher, I shall not attempt to discuss the problem of historical causation. There is an interesting symposium on this question in the *Journal of the History of Ideas*, III (1942), 3-50. Historians are seldom entirely satisfied with their efforts to discover causal relations, but they would insist that historical events do not occur in a completely haphazard way, and that certain events could not have occurred unless other events had preceded them.

complicated and often obscure; there is usually a great temptation to oversimplify them or to seize on surface explanations which merely state the problem in new terms. Laymen are especially likely to fall into the second error—to say, for example, that the Roman Empire fell because the Romans were degenerate. Professional historians are less apt to be superficial, but in digging deeper they can become even more narrow in their interpretation. As Professor Heaton points out in his essay, explanations of historical events based entirely on economic factors are seldom entirely convincing, even though they are the result of prolonged research, and the same objection may be made to any system of historical causation based on study of only one type of activity.

The historian cannot legitimately evade this problem of massing and linking together his facts. If he does, he becomes a mere dealer in intellectual antiques, who heaps together materials which will be arranged and used by others. Only when the past has a pattern does it have meaning, and if the historian cannot find the pattern men who are less skillful or less honest will make it for him. Only a tiny fraction of the population can draw sound historical conclusions from a mass of raw facts, and even this fraction can do it for only a few limited topics. We are all laymen in most fields of history, and if those fields are to be of any use to us someone must simplify and arrange the facts. Even in our daily life we cannot make decisions without drawing on a stock of generalizations which we have built up from the facts of our own personal history. It would be an intolerable burden if we had to review the details of all past purchases before deciding to trade with a certain store, or all our former conversations with a friend before inviting him to dinner. If formal history is to widen and deepen our own personal experience, if it is to be a guide to action and not an escape from reality, it must make generalizations and draw conclusions.

The scholar who will not do this for fear of being inaccurate is guilty of the greatest inaccuracy of all—he is saying, in effect, that history has no value, except to the specialist. We all know better than that. The value of history, like the existence of free will, cannot be proved —it is simply a basic fact of human experience. We all believe that the past explains the present and forecasts the future—not in the crude sense of an absolute duplication of events, but in the sense that there will always be familiar elements in a new situation which will aid us in making decisions and in judging what the results of those decisions will be. The wider and deeper our experience the greater our chances of recognizing these familiar elements, and history, properly written, can increase our stock of experiences many fold. We may go wrong in following the clues which it offers, but we would be lost without them. No one could stand the strain of beginning each day in a new world in which there was no rational basis for any decision and no way of predicting the results of any action. History, even at its worst, gives us the comforting and necessary feeling that the world is stable and intelligible. History at its best gives us a real chance of reacting sensibly to a new situation. It does not guarantee the correctness of our response, but it should improve the quality of our judgment.

A rough parallel may be found in certain card games. There is almost no chance that one distribution of cards will be repeated in a subsequent deal in bridge. Yet a man who has played several thousand hands of bridge should be able to make intelligent decisions and predictions even though every deal presents a new situation. He should be able to use his high cards and long suits effectively; he should be able to make some shrewd guesses about the location of cards in other hands. Not every experienced player will develop these skills. Some men are unable to generalize from their past experience, and others cannot see analogies between the present and the past. But, generally speaking, the experienced player will make better use of his cards than the man who has played only ten hands. There is such a thing as card sense, developed from long experience. There is also such a thing as a sense of the realities and possibilities of social activity, which can be developed from a study of the proper sort of history.

It is in acquiring, or seeking to acquire, this sense of social realities that the historian ceases to be a scientist and becomes an artist. In criticizing source material, in establishing the truth of individual facts there are certain rules which can be applied almost automatically. A papal letter, supposedly of the fourth century, which uses the formula "*servus servorum Dei*" is probably a forgery, since the phrase was not used by the popes of the period. A pamphlet issued by a government to justify a declaration of war must be used with great caution, since no government has ever printed all the relevant material in such a situation. But there is no automatic way of checking the accuracy of historical generalizations or statements about causal relationships. An historian may be extremely careful about the truth of each individual fact, he may guard himself scrupulously against prejudice, and yet his conclusions may be misleading. Accuracy and honesty by themselves will not enable a man to understand the past, or to present the record of human experience in a usable and useful form. The historian must be accurate and honest, but he must also possess sympathy, imagination, and understanding. These are qualities which cannot be learned like chemical formulae or reasoned out like geometrical theorems. They can be acquired only through long years of study and reflection, through the example of wise and understanding teachers, through the reading of books which stir the imagination. The student may be shown the terrible complexity of the problem, but he cannot be taught the solution. In the long run his ability to write history will depend on his ability to profit from his own experience, which is only to say that a man must understand his own history before he attempts to understand the history of others.

It is easier to describe the qualities of good historical writing than it is to tell anyone how they may be acquired. Good historical writing is distinguished, above everything else, by a sense of balance and proportion. There must be a balance between the familiar and the strange, between the importance given to individual effort and to great social trends, between the influence ascribed to thought and to action. The writer who cannot keep these proportions fairly even will not only mislead his readers, he will also bore them.

There must be a balance between the familiar and the strange because the concept of continuity and change is the basis of all historical thinking. If the essential elements of human nature and human institutions never changed there would be no point in studying history—a few years of practical experience would teach everyone all that he needed to know. If, on the other hand, human nature and human institutions changed completely with every decade or every generation the study of history would be equally useless, since it would have no points of contact with existing realities. But our lives are based on the assumption that, while change is inevitable, it will never be complete—that there will always be some familiar elements in a new situation. There is a sound instinct in most students and readers of history which leads them to reject the work of historians who depart too far from this assumption. If the past is described in terms of the present it becomes a pale, unsatisfactory imitation of real life. If the past is described as if it had occurred on another planet, it becomes a fantasy, and not a very good one at that, since it is bound to be contaminated by some reference to reality.

This lack of balance is especially common and especially dangerous in dealing with the earlier periods of European history. In the Middle Ages the principle of continuity and change can be completely obscured by overemphasis on the peculiar nature of medieval beliefs and customs. Properly handled, study of the Middle Ages stimulates the historical imagination more than that of any other period. The student sees men who have all the normal human passions and interests responding to ideas which have little influence today. He sees institutions which are an essential part of our civilization arising in a society very unlike our own. He sees that a successful response to the need for social organization can be built on assumptions which we reject, and that human nature, if not changeable, is at least more flexible than some dogmatists are willing to admit. The student who limits himself to the history of the last two centuries is like a novice card player whose teacher has given him only hands with normal distribution. Study of earlier periods is essential if the unusual combinations which have occurred in the past and which may occur again in the future are to be understood. But all these values are lost if the Middle Ages are described either as a poor imitation of modern civilization, or as a period in which men were so childish or so saintly that they were unaware of the actual needs of organized society.

Balance between the importance of individuals and the importance of social trends is even harder to attain. Everyone who has ever written a biography is aware of the danger of making his hero more important and influential than he actually was. Everyone who has worked with the history of political or economic institutions is aware of the danger of ascribing to these institutions a power of autonomous development which is not dependent on individual effort. Both extremes contradict the facts of ordinary experience and obscure the values inherent in the study of history. In actual life we know that individual decisions may be of the utmost importance, and that the man who merely drifts with the current of events is apt to wind up in obscurity or disaster. We know, on the other hand, that there are general trends which must be considered in making any individual decision and which often rule out certain courses of action. Mere awareness of these trends, however, will not automatically solve our social problems. The general tendencies of a society furnish a framework within which decisions must be made, but the decisions are made by individuals and not by abstractions labeled "Law," "Religion," "Capital" and the like. Even the Marxists, who have pushed the theory of economic determinism to its extreme limit, have had to reserve a place for individual effort. They do not believe capitalism will automatically evolve into socialism; rather, they feel that the decisive change can be brought about only by the desperate efforts of a minority of determined individuals. The assertion of the necessity of revolution is an assertion of the necessity of individual decision.

The study of history reinforces our almost instinctive belief in the equal importance of individual effort and general social trends. We see that widespread economic or social change can create problems which demand an immediate answer, but these social and economic changes do not dictate the answers which may be given. The individual may not have an unlimited range of choice, but he always has at least two choices, and the cumulative effect of a series of individual decisions may be enormous. The classic example is the different development of English and French institutions. Here are two countries which had almost identical experiences, which were closely associated politically and culturally for many centuries, and which nevertheless developed very different types of government and very different economic activities. The fact that England had a William the Conqueror when France had a Philip I, the fact that France had a Richelieu when England had a Buckingham, may explain some of these differences. Yet it is as dangerous to overemphasize the importance of individuals as to explain everything in terms of impersonal social forces. History becomes flat and lifeless if it is written exclusively in terms of great men. If the great men are isolated from the society of which they were a part, they become so much alike that they are not very interesting. Plutarch's *Lives* and many modern biographies share this weakness. The reader becomes a little weary of hearing the same strong character and the same lovable and harmless eccentricities described over and over again. On the other hand, if history is written in a purely deterministic vein it becomes valueless. The machine grinds on and on; complicated societies build themselves up automatically and break down of their own weight, and nobody can do anything about it. A roller-coaster offers an intensified form of the same sensations at the cost of much less effort.

Finally, there is the need for balancing the influence

of ideas and actions. This is the place where the historian finds it most difficult to distinguish between cause and effect. It is perfectly clear, to take one example, that political theories are always developed to justify an existing set of political facts. It is equally clear that a political theory, once developed, is an extraordinarily hard thing to kill. It will live on for centuries and men will make desperate efforts to force new political facts into conformity with the old theory. It is certain that actual conditions never correspond fully to existing political, economic, or religious theories. And yet a society which has no ideals, no standards, and no goals is a society which is ready to disintegrate. Life must have meaning if men are to make the sacrifices which are necessary to secure wholehearted cooperation, and life is given meaning by the great ideas which are developed in crucial periods. The historian must recognize the power of ideas. They are just as much facts of social experience as forms of government or means of production; in many cases, they are the most important facts about the society which is being studied. At the same time, it is an error to assume that they are entirely autonomous, that they are not affected by purely physical activities. There are many political histories which are unsatisfactory because they do not allow sufficient importance to ideas, but there are just as many intellectual histories which are meaningless because they discuss ideas as if they operated in a vacuum. A history of Europe which failed to recognize the effects of religious beliefs on political events would not make sense. A history of religious beliefs which left out the social and political background would leave the reader with a feeling that theologians were a rather peculiar group of people who enjoyed raising unnecessary issues.

It is evident that this balance among the different elements in historical thinking is difficult to attain. Is there any chance that the historian can reach his goal, that he can know enough about all the factors involved to give the proper weight to each? On the purely mechanical side, conditions are all in his favor. As a result of the efforts of generation after generation of scholars, we have an abundance of source material which illustrates every aspect of social activity. The old overemphasis on political materials is practically ended; intellectual history, economic history, art history, social history have been given a fair share, or even more than a fair share of attention in recent years. Historians are becoming more and more interested in the study of whole civilizations and this has forced them to think more about the problem of balance and proportion. At the same time the constant testing of old hypotheses and the multiplication of new ones have effectively discredited simple, unilinear explanations of complex historical phenomena. This work has made the historian aware of the many forces which operate in human society, it has made him realize that there is usually more than one cause for any important event, and it has forced him to consider all aspects of human life in his attempt to understand the past.

The essential limitation is now the mind of the historian, rather than the materials which are available for study. This limitation can never be entirely overcome, for no human mind can ever grasp all the factors involved in a given social situation. Yet there is no reason to despair simply because we cannot achieve perfection. Historians once felt inferior because they could not speak with the certainty of the natural scientist, but no reputable scientist will now claim that he has reached, or has any hope of reaching, absolute truth. He will merely say that he has found ways of building working hypotheses which enable him to make intelligent use of certain factors in his environment. Every statesman—even every successful politician—has likewise had to make working hypotheses about the nature of his own society and to stake his reputation and his political life on their approximate accuracy. A good historian should be able to do at least as well. Many scholars would affirm, with Professor Holborn, "the validity of the results" obtained "through the critical and systematic approach to history." A man who has spent years in studying a particular period, in soaking himself in all the available records, should develop a feeling for that period which will enable him to come fairly close to understanding the social and intellectual forces which were operating at the time. No historian believes that he will ever know the whole truth about any episode in the past, but it should be possible for us to come a good deal nearer the truth than any of our predecessors. The historian who has both knowledge and wisdom, accuracy and insight, should be able to develop hypotheses which are both useful and usable. If all our historical writing could come up to the level of our best historical writing, we could profit from the experience of our ancestors as no previous generation has ever done.

Even if he cannot reach this level, the honest and conscientious historian will have something to contribute. History is almost the only academic study which still deals with the facts of ordinary experience, which still dares appeal to common sense. Both the sciences and the arts have turned away from external reality and have become more and more involved in the study of abstract concepts. The scientists of an earlier period could draw diagrams of the world as they saw it; now they must express their theories in elaborate mathematical formulae. Science has given up the attempt to represent the world in visual terms and is seeking only satisfactory intellectual concepts which will accommodate a host of lesser abstractions. The arts and literature have also shown a tendency to turn away from the visible world and to seek refuge in the hidden depths of the subconscious. Even the sister studies of politics and economics are trying to escape the problem of dealing with specific individuals and situations by reducing everything to statistical tables and mathematical formulae. The historian may be accused of dealing only with the surface of things while his colleagues and competitors seek the inner truth. The historian can only answer that he is dealing with life as the ordinary individual sees it and that for the practical conduct of affairs we must act as if the visible, external world were the ultimate reality. Some one must try to make sense out of the world of direct experience and the historian's great opportunity comes from the fact that other scholars have abandoned the task as hopeless.

It is this closeness to ordinary life which gives history its interest and its influence, just as it is this closeness to ordinary life which is most apt to lead the historian into errors of interpretation and judgment. The historian is not living in a world of his own creation; he must still test all his work by the standards of common sense, and the common sense of one generation is apt to seem somewhat eccentric to the next. Thus, our own age is apt to think that economic interest is the most obvious motive for men of any period and the historian who is not careful may find himself overemphasizing the profit motive in his study of the past. This danger can never be entirely eliminated, though the more thorough the historian's knowledge of any special period the less apt he is to read present interests into it. But, great as the danger is, it is compensated by the advantage which the historian has in dealing with the world of ordinary experience rather than with the worlds of rational, sub-rational, or supra-rational abstractions. He can still talk the language of the ordinary man and, if he knows his job, he can communicate with and influence the ordinary man directly. The scientist needs an interpreter and is often very much annoyed by the quality of the interpreter's work. The historian should be able to speak to his own generation face to face.

The historians who are represented in this volume have dealt with the problem of communicating history to the ordinary man in different ways. Professor Barzun is concerned with the question of the gap between scholarly history and the history which is remembered and used by the average citizen. Professor Holborn, in illustrating his concept of the "science of history," describes the principles which inspired two great historians and the values which they found in their work. Professor Heaton discusses the impact of the economic interpretation of history on historians, and uses this example to warn against overemphasizing any single aspect of social activity. Professor Malone stresses the danger of drowning individual achievements in a foggy sea of social forces, and points out the obstacles which make biography one of the most difficult forms of history. Professor LaPiana shows the danger of trying to fit history to a pattern imposed by non-historical beliefs. They all feel that history is a humanizing, if not necessarily a humanistic study, that when it is properly treated it can enable us to act more intelligently in the world of today, but that unless it is written with wisdom and understanding, honesty and sympathy, imagination and insight, it will be of no avail.

HISTORY, POPULAR AND UNPOPULAR

By JACQUES BARZUN

History, Popular and Unpopular

IN a great essay entitled *The Use and Harm of History*, Nietzsche contrasts Man with the happy animal in the fields, which lives ignorant of its past. Man, on the contrary, and particularly modern man is, according to Nietzsche, weighed down and crippled by his sense of the past, by history. The distinction is striking—it had struck Schopenhauer before Nietzsche —and it at once commends itself: man differs from the animals in this at least, that his memory reaches back farther over his own experience and that of his race, and retains a product called history. But if we believe many a writer of our times, of whom Mr. John Dos Passos is the most recent, the ordinary American of today is in the position of the happy animal in the fields; he has no sense of history. The Spanish philosopher Ortega y Gasset makes the same observation about modern man in general, and in his *Revolt of the Masses* he describes a new type of plebeian springing up all over the world as one who has been "emptied of his own history."[1]

The natural result of these observations is an attempt to pour back a little history into the mass-man or the American, as the case may be; and so we see books appearing on every hand which, like Mr. Dos Passos's

[1] cf. his more recent book, *Toward a Philosophy of History*, N.Y. 1941, in which our epoch is characterized as having "lost its memory and returned to infancy." p. 243.

volume, *The Ground We Stand On*, try to make us
aware of our tradition. Sometimes they try to make us
understand the tradition of our enemies, who in these
days are found under every bush. In either case, the
beneficial use of history is an accepted article of faith,
Mr. Dos Passos going so far as to say that in ordinary
times history has a merely ornamental use, whereas in
times of troubles like our own its cultivation becomes
imperative.

At the same time, other writers, notably Mr. H. G.
Wells, are inclined to blame the historical notions we
do have for the mental disorder and distress in which
we find ourselves. There are too many traditions—so
runs the argument—we remember too much and are
too unwilling to forget old precedents, old grudges, old
ways of life and thought. This is what holds back the
mind of the world at a time when science and technology have spurted ahead and revolutionized material
life. It is the "poison called history" which perpetuates
misunderstandings and animosities in situations where
what we need is a fresh start and the cancelling out of
past wrongs. These critics stress the harm of history,
ascribing to it the very evils that the other group would
cure by an even greater dose of the poison. Nietzsche,
as usual, gives due weight to both arguments and over-
comes the contradiction by a formula of his own which
does not concern us here.

What does concern us is to clear up a certain ambiguity in this debate in order once again to take stock of
history, its powers and its problems, and so decide how

to use it as a discipline. For it is certain that if we simply follow the drift of our old routines, reading or producing any type of history at random, we shall be left in the same state of confusion that has been termed the "contemporary chaos," if not "the decline of the West." The warnings and prophecies in our ears are too bewildering for a casual glance to resolve into order and, as in the present dispute concerning history itself, the rival claims are too contradictory to be accepted or dismissed on the strength of mere hunches.

I have spoken of a certain ambiguity in the debates about history. Everyone will have noticed that in all European languages the word "history" is used for two distinct things—events in themselves and the record of those events. Thus we say that a prime minister makes history and that a scholar or journalist writes it. This ambiguity deceives no one and it is worth noting only as a reminder that from the moment a so-called event is past, our knowledge of it depends upon some go-between, some form of hearsay. We do not, in other words, come into direct contact with any but the slightest portion of history, that slightest portion being the substance of our individual lives. And even there direct contact is fleeting and its force kept alive only by memory.

But this aspect of the distinction between history-as-event and history-as-recollection leads us to another, more important ambiguity calling for a second distinction. We must distinguish between history as it exists in the minds of men and history as it exists on the shelves of libraries; we must mark a difference between popular history and what I shall not blush to call Unpopular History. Popular history is the living remnant of tradition in the minds of the majority. It is a commonplace that the spirit of nationality which characterizes the modern epoch is based on the possession of a common language, common customs, and common historical traditions. However stupid or uneducated, the most indifferent citizen will remember and respond to certain ideas connected with his country's past. It may be a picture of Abraham Lincoln's log cabin or it may be the two words Monroe Doctrine—these symbols are popular history in the sense that they call up at once a series of compelling beliefs about the past. As Mary Baker Eddy declared in a public advertisement, "I believe strictly in the Monroe Doctrine, in our Constitution, and in the laws of God."[2] Lincoln's log cabin may suggest the heroism of western pioneers or it may mean that humble birth is no bar to high office. To others it probably "proves" that only the workingman has political wisdom or that bodily strength is a guarantee of honesty. But even these suppositions of mine are too precise and abstract to indicate the force of a tradition when it is clothed in historical symbols that pass current. With their proper names and specific virtues, these images are powers risen from the dead. They become, as we say, a part of the language, and all political action, whether democratic or demagogic, re-

[2] Published on the hundredth anniversary of the Monroe Doctrine; quoted in Dexter Perkins, *Hands Off, a History of the Monroe Doctrine*, Boston, 1941, p. ix.

quires their use. History thereby becomes the strongest, most direct means of communication between man and man. To a Frenchman you need not explain Joan of Arc. The intricate details of her career, trial, and death are as nothing compared with the image that spells patriotism, kingship, and sainthood. To many an American the Monroe Doctrine and the words "no entangling alliances" mean respectively "Hands off" and "Nothing doing" as sufficient answers to all future problems; and this in spite of the fact that a scholar must spend half a lifetime understanding the complexities of the Monroe Doctrine or that the words "no entangling alliances" were actually never uttered by George Washington.

Popular history is thus the ground on which the two opposing groups of publicists contend. It is on that common ground that historical ideas become potent and possibly dangerous. The issue is whether we can add to the contents of popular history and at the same time enlighten the bearers of it, or whether we had not better declare a moratorium on history and wipe the slate as nearly clean as possible. For although the unity of modern nations is based on common historical traditions, every such tradition is also split into regional, class, religious or other sub-traditions that compel belief in the same manner, though usually in opposite directions. We have seen with our own eyes the effect of these cross-currents in the split which contributed in part to the defeat of France. Republican *versus* Royalist, the French people has for 150 years been divided by the revolution of 1789, and this inextinguishable civil war has more than once decided the fate of the country. Nor is this division peculiar to any one people. Everywhere social groups differ not only in their present interests but in their historical memories, all of which are one-sided. While British industry looks back on the glory of having been the workshop of the world, trade-unionists think of the Tolpuddle Martyrs; while the India Office congratulates itself upon the reforms of Morley and Minto, Hindus remember General Dyer and the Amritsar Massacre. Who can doubt that in this country many practical problems in the South, problems of agriculture, industry, education, racial relations and individual psychology, could be better solved if by magic the memory of the Civil War could be effaced and the same difficulties looked upon as wholly new?

That this making of all things new is impossible, proves the incurably historical nature of man and brings us to the only possible mode of improvement: the overhauling of our habits of historical thought, which in turn means a complete change from our humdrum ways of reading, writing, and talking history. But before new ways can be indicated, it is necessary to understand something of present practice. If we go beyond the evident confusion that prevails in popular history, what are its characteristics? The first is that it is concrete and simple. Just as the common man will not listen to philosophical doubts about the evidence of his senses, so he is impatient of arguments about historical matters. The Monroe Doctrine means "Hands off"; Lincoln was a man of the people who rose by sheer merit; the sinking of the *Lusitania* was an act of wanton aggression: these are the positions taken by the common man as historian. In the second place, popular history is discontinuous: between the blowing up of the *Maine* and the sinking of the *Lusitania*, there are no affronts to the national honor. More than that, there are no affronts by our nation to the honor of others—the treatment of the Chinese during the Boxer rebellion, or of the Philippines about the same time, figure little or not at all in the popular mind. This is of course the heaviest argument for those who denounce history. History fosters national egotism and distorts the reality of human affairs. National or sectarian, popular history is always constructed on partisan lines. It is a record of our prowess and our grievances, for it draws its concreteness and simplicity from a perpetual reduction of world history to the scale of the uncritical ego.

This process of identification is natural and up to a point indispensable. But its practical drawbacks are only too clear. A nation is not only a human group possessing a common past; it is one that has to share a common future. But if national policy is hemmed in at every turn by the common man's complacency and timid simplification of experience, that future is bound to be, or to seem, chaotic. Popular history makes no provision for the future otherwise than by hoping to duplicate the past. Every precedent is sacred, every novelty is suspect; surface similarities deceive into security, and surface differences mislead into unnecessary panic and despair. But since memory cannot be abolished, how can old formulas from the past yield new ones for grasping and shaping the future? This question leads us into the heart of our inquiry by forcing us to ask what the sources of these old formulas really are and whether they are amenable to change.

The sources of popular history are two in number: the textbooks used in the schools and popular literature. In this latter category, I include newspapers and periodicals—especially the photographic—historical and other novels, "readable" biographies and histories, and moving pictures. It is legitimate, I think, to omit from this list a source of history which in the past would have come first, namely oral tradition. The days of the grandfather recounting historical events to his progeny are past. The progeny either does not want to hear or else obtains a comparable satisfaction from printed or filmed matter. This difference between Western man today and the man of the Middle Ages or the Zuñi Indian is important. It means that popular history is more and more a by-product of Unpopular History, that is, of scholarship. Schoolbooks are based, directly or indirectly, on scholarly works; the mass of cheap biographies and histories likewise filters down from above; the motion picture industry hires experts to see that Henry VIII appears in the correct costume; magazines like *Time* and *Life* go through elaborate rituals to verify their accounts of persons and places that break into notoriety; the modern reporter or radio commentator is an historian *sans le savoir*, and everyone who is overtaken by flood, war, or pestilence records his impressions on the spot. In short, the historical attitude is dominant and universal, the age is historical down to the roots. Why, then, the complaint about the insufficiency of popular history? Because this abundance is undigested, unproductive, a passing show. As in the famous patter song, we "take all the remarkable people in history and rattle them off to a popular tune," and so we should not be surprised that the "residuum" is nothing more enlightened than a heavy dragoon.

This paradox, that we wallow in historical matter without developing the historical sense, calls for an analysis of the sources of supply. This can be done here only in the briefest way and I must rely on your own experience for illustrations of the generic[3] faults of scholarship, textbook writing, and so-called popularizations, which together form the reservoir of history-as-consciousness. And first about schoolbooks. Even those who can remember no history can remember their feelings about it, for it is a subject which shares with mathematics the privilege of an all-or-none allegiance. People who meet an historian at dinner invariably break the ice with one of two remarks: "History! I think it's so fascinating." Or else, "History! It was my worst subject. I must be very stupid but I never could remember dates." It is usually impossible to change these convictions by telling the first of these persons that what he enjoyed was probably a feat of word-juggling having little to do with historical intelligence; and by

[3] I do not of course mean every instance of each genre. There are brilliant exceptions to all my strictures, but not enough of them.

telling the other that his—or rather, her—capacity for remembering the secret history of her friends is an historical performance in itself. For a second aspect of the paradox before us is that although the untrained mind tends to reduce history to individual proportions, it does not fashion for itself images sufficiently mixed to resemble even the simplest reality. And for this state of impotence I believe that the conventions of the textbook are largely responsible.

A textbook is intended for a very large public which is peculiar in that it cannot make its own choices. Teachers and school boards choose for the young and the young must like it or lump it. It is hard to see how this arrangement can be superseded, but it is not hard to see how it leads to a certain artificiality in the textbooks themselves. Most of them combine an attitude of talking down to the pupil with a show of scholarly completeness addressed to the teacher. Schoolbooks are thus crammed with facts—if they are not, those that seem fuller crowd them out of the market. Still, there are limits to the number of pages which students can be asked to read in any one course, and consequently each of these "facts" is reduced to its skeleton form, is deprived of its unique character and made into a standardized item, to be learned by an effort of memory agreeable only to those who have a knack for it. This is what is meant by the complaint that history is all dates. The objectors are wrong about the actual contents of history; they are right about the impression which it makes on them: it is *as if* all the facts were as disembodied and unrelated as dates. Recall the tone of So-and-So's textbook: it was impersonal and uniform, and men and events always fell into a few ready-made categories expressed by simple adjectives. For example, prime ministers who succeed are always shrewd; those that do not are either incompetent or idealistic. Kings are good or bad; the good ones continually drain marshes and build roads; occasionally they reorganize the finances or promulgate a code of laws. Bad kings are weak-minded or dissolute, and so on. I need not multiply examples, for I am sure many of you have read that perfect critique of textbook writing which is called *1066 and All That*. Note that it gives the minimum of English history left over, not in the mind of the great masses, but in the minds of people who have repeatedly studied the subject without ever possessing it.

In students who reach college and who thus have just undergone a long exposure to this sterilized and packaged reality, the lack of historical sense finds expression in two phrases. One is "in those days"—meaning: people and things in the past were strange and inexplicable; we have to learn about them by rote. The other phrase is: "that was nothing but"—something else, meaning: any action in the past can be reduced to the one most obvious reason that I, as a cynical youth, can think of. And so by another twist of the same paradox we have noted, that part of the past which does indeed resemble our present is felt to be utterly foreign, because textbook humanity consists of puppets; and that part which perhaps differs most from the youthful reader's limited experience is seen as the outcome of callow motives, because the puppets must be endowed with some sort of mainspring.

So much for textbooks, that great source of popular history in nations where education is free, public, and compulsory. I shall return later to the ways in which both teachers and books could theoretically be lifted from this double rut of abstraction and melodrama. We must now pay attention to scholarship, for although it seldom if ever comes into direct contact with the public mind, its tone and temper and methods, as we have seen, can affect all derivative historiography. Scholars have been too often praised and criticized to care much about what the general public think of them. The adjective *dryasdust* continues to be applied to their work although they know perfectly well that their subject is not dust to their touch and that many a novel is drier than a good monograph. They feel thus, not because they are abnormal creatures, but because their interest in a portion of the past is genuine, though doubtless uncommon. There is in judging of our fellow man's occupations a native intolerance that is appalling; our egotism making us forget that nothing is futile or deadly in itself, but in its relation to some thinking mind. The lowbrow who despises the archivist is probably himself a student of baseball biography and race-track history, and to that extent a highbrow. For history is all-inclusive—the past of cattle-breeding or of chess, of insurance or lace-making, is a branch of history, and its students are all equally entitled to their specialties. Whence it follows that no historical subject is dry, however exhaustively and minutely it is treated, provided it is really a subject and it is really treated.

I must explain what I mean by these two provisos. By a subject which is not fit for treatment I refer to a class of speculations about matters which it would be interesting to know but which it is clearly impossible to ascertain. I believe a good deal of mistrust has grown around scholarship from its attempts to trace the early wanderings of the Germanic tribes or to establish the identity of the Man in the Iron Mask. The evidence for the conclusions advanced is not ample enough, which means that every effort to piece the scraps together is nearly as plausible and as inconclusive as every other. Sir Thomas Browne rightly says that the "song the sirens sang and the name that Achilles assumed when he hid among the women are not beyond conjecture" but scholars should remember that conjecture is a pastime, not a duty.

This lack of proportion and unwillingness to stop guessing, however, are often confused with a very different function of the historian. Outsiders are apt to mistake a task that obviously spells drudgery for one that is absurd or unimportant. To many people bibliographies are foolish and bibliographies of bibliographies the height of comedy. And yet they can see without laughter men engaged in moving a pile of stones from one place to another more convenient. Indeed this comparison does scant justice to the many gifts required of a bibliographer, even though one must admit that these gifts do not belong to the highest order. No, the recurrent error of scholarship does not consist in devoting itself to preparatory tasks. It consists in forgetting what these tasks are preparatory to. And it is not the scholarly drudge who forgets it: the man who prepares a concordance or who edits a text fully expects that people less learned than he will use it and save time in finding what they want. The historian who forgets his duty is the one who attempts the treatment of an actual historical question and thinks he has achieved it when he has only rummaged into the past and exhibited his finds. This is what I mean by a subject not being really treated. In this country the Ph.D. dissertation is the best opportunity for committing this kind of error. Under the timid guidance of a teacher who may or may not be a practiced writer, the student collects a quantity of facts, verified and more or less relevant, and then publishes them in a series of formless chapters that only his sponsor and his examination committee can read. It would be hard to exaggerate the harm arising from this neglect of composition: the young historian comes to think of his work as the tracking down of data, and of publication as a routine matter of transcribing notes. Nor can he be excused by saying that here are the materials for a future historian's use. These are not bare materials but materials spoiled. Nobody can use what has been ill-expressed and ill-arranged, for the whole meaning of history consists in the proper delineation and the proper arrangement of its component "facts." The meaning is in the atmosphere as much as in the words, between the lines as much as within them. And if the next worker in the field is unable to build upon such rubbly foundations, all the more is the general reader convinced that history is both beyond and beneath him.

It remains to examine the chief types of historical writing that is intended to be popular, works neither imposed on their readers like textbooks, nor limited to an expert audience like scholarship. Let us begin with the movies. Here, as I have said, the attempt to be exact is painful and intense. The country is apparently full of persons who will detect trifling errors and write indignant letters to Hollywood. So we may be relatively sure that Henry VIII's table manners will be true to his period and that George Washington will wear the right wig. What is not so sure is that the purport of the action will make historical sense, regardless of the interpretation chosen. For example, in Mr. George Arliss's impersonation of Voltaire, that historical figure was shown writing a pamphlet of which the immediate result was to provoke a riot in his own street; he was shown gloating behind the curtains of his room as he saw a mob wrecking a shop on the opposite side. Presumably this invention expressed the commonplace that the writings of Voltaire led to the French revolution. But this shorthand representation is a little too rapid. For one thing, Voltaire never wrote incendiary tracts addressed to the man in the street; and for another, although he once predicted a revolution in France, his whole temper was set against insurrection and violence. We have here a good instance of the way nuances are destroyed by popularization. And yet it is precisely this type of nuance that any useful populariza-

tion should inculcate. It should combat the melo-
dramatic notions we are born with and replace them
with a truer feeling for the variety and inconsistency
of human character. This does not mean that the
movie-goer must be swamped with ifs and buts, but
rather that our ready-made conceptions should be
stretched by the addition of a few unexpected traits,
closer to the complexity of life.

The moving pictures belong in this respect under
the general category of journalism, a profession whose
faults are not—as is often said—sensationalism and nov-
elty-hunting but on the contrary the adroit aping of
sensation and novelty. I was very forcibly struck by this
fact some years ago when a large New England newspaper decided to send as special reporter to the seat of
a murder trial a person having no journalistic standing
or experience, but a modest and recognized literary
ability. The resulting pair of daily reports in the same
newspaper, one by a regular staff-member and the other
by this outsider, revealed an even sharper contrast than
might have been expected. It was not merely that the
outsider avoided the cliches which make every murder
case sound like every other; it was also that the non-
professional mind perceived actual differences of fact.
I recall one instance in which every newspaper in the
town declared that the accused had broken down
"under severe grilling by the district attorney." The
other observer reported on the contrary that the prisoner when first brought in had collapsed, but that after
being restored he had stood up firmly under the questions of the prosecutor. Now as a piece of contemporary

history, it should seem as if the latter were the true novelty. But journalistic tradition has it, rightly or wrongly, that the public wants a *regular* sensation and a *familiar* novelty, so that by joint force of habit, the facts must be twisted to answer the general expectation.[4]

As everyone knows, it is this same journalistic attitude which infects the lower order of popular history and biography. The frame of mind is accurately conveyed by the adjectives it uses: the simplest things are invariably "curious," "amazing," "thrilling," "astonishing," "extraordinary." The author seems to have been born but a few days before writing his book. Yet at the same time that these words are employed, the characters and situations themselves are unconsciously deformed to fit stock patterns. That this is no recognition of the unchanging stuff of human life, is shown by the fact that a very few historical subjects enjoy preeminent favor. They are considered intrinsically more exciting than all the rest. Thus Mary Queen of Scots is historical subject No. 1, with Henry VIII and Lord Byron running close seconds. Publishers never tire of issuing new works about them and the blurbs press this never-failing spring. In the announcement of a sober work on John Knox, I found this concession to the taste I am describing: "We would remind the reader that this historical study inevitably deals with Mary Queen of Scots."[5] The simple truth is that popular history and

[4] cf. in G. B. Shaw's *The Doctor's Dilemma* the scene in which the newspaper reporter takes down the words of the dying artist.

[5] Catalogue of the "Life and Letters" Series, under Edwin Muir's *John Knox*, 1931, p. 5 of the advertisement section.

biography run in grooves as well marked as those of popular fiction; and this is of course its condemnation as an agent for developing the historical sense, since in history the mind must be prepared for every possible and improbable truth and the wits sharpened to see it.

Above this journalism in book form come two categories of popularization of lesser scope but greater influence. One is the "official publication" by a public or private body upon matters supposed to be of general interest. A good example is the Congressional Committee's publication in 1937 of a small handbook commemorating the 150th anniversary of the Constitution. When I say a good example, I mean also a bad one; in short, an excellent opportunity missed. Though dedicated to the 128 million people who want to know about the Constitution, this little work erred in assuming that so large a public could be reached by the appeal of documents. As it stands, the volume is of slight use to anybody. Scholars do not need it, for its contents are available in better form elsewhere; and non-scholars will either throw it away after a casual glance or store it with similar lumber issued by state and county commissions, banks, insurance companies, and manufacturers. All these publications might be termed "perfunctory history" and their defect comes down to an inability to decide who the likely reader is going to be and how to keep his attention. Original documents and the storybook style do not belong under the same covers. As for the catechism method so often employed, it may amuse children, but asking adults "How many words are there in the Declaration of

Independence and how long does it take to read?"
does not stimulate but narcotizes the historical sense.[6]

The second type of ambitious popularization—the
books written for the "general educated reader"—are
at the present time very numerous and possibly influential. They reach the really living segment of national
opinion, the people who join habits of reflection with
executive responsibility and whose base for decision
cannot be too broad. The book by Mr. Dos Passos
which I mentioned before belongs in this category and
it is unfortunate that I must single it out for the short-
comings of its class rather than praise it as a triumph.
The Ground We Stand On was an admirable subject
for a great writer such as Mr. Dos Passos undoubtedly
is, and to have conceived it as a succession of large biographical essays was a fine stroke. Nor did the author
rush in unprepared. His research was full and conscientious. Wherein, then, has he failed? Simply in suppos-
ing that what he found interesting after months of
research would, in chronicle style and without solid
interpretation, equally interest his readers. The result
is that as we read we find no unifying principle, no
lighting up of single facts by coherent thought, no link
except the most fitful with what we may know or think
about. We are left inconclusively holding a bag of
notes. The book lacking form, we notice that the
amount of detail about secondary figures is as great as
that about primary ones; that the quotations from
original documents are overlong and duplicated by

[6] Condensed from the questionnaire in the volume under
consideration, p. 165.

paraphrase; and that even the language of the narrative is uncertain and swings from slang phrases to textbook formulas.

It must be said in palliation of these faults that Mr. Dos Passos is a beginner in the art of historical composition. Most professional historians have the advantage of making their first essay in the utter obscurity of the Ph.D. thesis. But it is interesting to note that Mr. Dos Passos's mastery as a novelist—an historical novelist at that—helped him relatively little. Though an artist, his errors are want of selection and want of pattern. He seems as if afraid to omit anything that he has found. If picturesque and true, why should any fact be rejected? Should not the historian limit the freedom which he enjoys as a novelist, and deal more "objectively" with true than with invented material? Yet if in the novel the central characters can carry the meaning of their world upon their sole shoulders, why is not the same true in a history that stresses individual endeavor? The literary art being common to both novel and history, what are the rules governing their respective presentation? These questions raise in effect the problem of the philosophy of history, and answering them will tie together the threads of this critique while leading us to some positive conclusions.

Obviously an historian cannot select arbitrarily. He has a responsibility toward something outside his private preference. Unless he is a mere collector, limiting himself to a very small subject and reporting everything he finds, he must have a criterion of choice, which implies a rationale of analysis and synthesis. Taken together, these form his philosophy. The term philosophy of history has long been in bad repute, for through abuse it has come to mean the forcible imposition of a creed upon the facts. I think the insidiousness of this kind of distortion has been exaggerated, but a mechanical bias is in any case not what I have in mind when I speak of a philosophy of history. What I do mean, the point and conclusion of this inquiry, consists of two parts. One concerns the nature of historiography, regardless of who the historian is; it expresses what I believe to be the consensus of my colleagues in this century. The other concerns my own view of the historian's art, that is to say of my own performance as an historian of ideas; it expresses my temperament. And I may add that any philosophy of history, implicit or explicit, can be broken down into these two components.

As regards the first part, then, I believe it is now agreed that the study of history supplies no answers to present riddles. There is no law of history, and no lesson in the literal sense of a dictum.[7] My friend Professor Robert Lynd when he lectured at Princeton some years ago was on this account rather scornful of history and advocated its elimination under the firm hand of the sociologists.[8] I have also heard him ask a candidate for a degree what theory of psychology the

[7] The most recent and fullest exposition of this view is Benedetto Croce's *History as the Story of Liberty*, N.Y., 1941.

[8] cf. Robert S. Lynd, *Knowledge for What?*, Princeton, 1939, pp. 13, 132ff, 174ff.

prospective historian held. And when the ingenuous youth declared, like the traveler at the customs, that he had none, Professor Lynd was confirmed in his opinion that history was a purposeless discipline, or rather, no discipline at all.

I agree with him in some of his strictures, but I reject his inference. Let me recall the distinction with which we started, between popular history, which is history in people's minds—and of course the channels it takes to reach them—and unpopular history, which is history on the bookshelf or in the minds of a few specialists. Now the fallacy of the sociologist's criticism is that he supposes the historian to aid mankind by the mere supplying of usable information. The sociologist is, with all due respect, a man seeking a recipe. He legitimately wants to know how to treat crime or prevent vagrancy or arrest the falling birthrate. His wisdom, if he has any, can be written down on a piece of paper and handed to someone else. Superficially the historian does the same thing: he tells us how bravely Washington endured at Valley Forge or how foolishly the Stuarts lost their throne. But the resemblance is an illusion. Historical examples are not formulas: we cannot be again in Washington's or the Stuarts' position, and it is not in transferable moral judgments that the worth of history consists. It is in the diagnostic power that it develops. Diagnostic power means seeing the familiar within the strange without losing the sense of either. History is not all strangeness nor all familiarity. It is as novel and as commonplace as life—which it recaptures—but with its pattern clearer and simpler by reason of our need for intelligibility. A student of history uses standard names for some of these recurrent patterns but he knows, for example, that when he speaks of a revolution he is not referring to a standard product, as uniform as graded eggs. To learn that historical events can never be dealt with in bunches, that the things we denote by identical names will not stack like coins of a single denomination, yet to recognize that the events of a given period or purport possess a family likeness—this is to be by way of developing a special sort of intelligence, properly called the historical reason. It is a skill akin to that of the practiced mariner, who does not forecast the weather merely from a red sunset or a mackerel sky but from all manner of signs combined in one intuitive operation.

This type of observation differs, of course, from the mathematico-physical reasoning we in this century are most inclined to admire. The historian indeed is no more a scientist than the navigator or the doctor. His historical reason, like their diagnostic power, is part subjective and part hypothetical, but its results are nonetheless tangible and true; not demonstrable like those of mathematics, but nonetheless usable by those willing to devote time to that long apprenticeship and meditation without which no historical work can be truly read or written. It might even be added that some of the great discoveries in physical science have themselves come about as a result of the same process of steeping, but in science the creative unreasoning reason is supplemented by an *ex post facto* demonstration that anyone can utilize without going through the first travail. The uncreative can learn the conclusions of a science and become a good enough technician, but the historian cannot skip his self-education. He who has merely learned the facts in an outline is only a crammed goose and not an historian.

The use of history is not external but internal. Not what you can do with history but what history does to you is its use. It is a personal discipline, not a measure of sanitation collectively applicable. That is why the problem of popular history is important and perennial, especially in a democracy. It is also why history has to be periodically rewritten. Many people imagine that this rewriting is needed because new facts have come to light—someone has found a packet of letters in an attic. If that were all, a few corrective footnotes to an established work would generally suffice. On the contrary, we require history written by our contemporaries whom we understand so that our minds may be filled and reshaped for dealing, not with a crisis once every ten years, but for dealing with life itself, every day; for spiritual balance, for political, artistic and social judgment, in a word for the conquest of provincialism—the provincialism of self, the provincialism of place, the provincialism of time.

Such being the use of history, it clearly implies that all history is ultimately intended to be read, to take effect somewhere, to unify past and present in someone's mind. What this should lead to in the practice of historiography is more subject to debate. But here again I think most historians are at one in rejecting any narrow, literal interpretation of usefulness or readability or relevance. We are all too familiar with histories built on an evolutionary plan which naively interprets the whole past as a mere preparation for the modern age; which systematically strains the evidence for germs of institutions or ideas which we find important, whether our ancestors found them so or not. This kind of history is pure Narcissism.[9] It discovers nothing and changes nothing. Not that the obvious present may not be a good point of departure. Mr. Dos Passos's project was excellent. We need not one but a dozen good studies of the liberal tradition. We likewise need books on dictatorships and revolutions; not, however, of the kind so frequent in these days, which try to prove that all our troubles come from Nietzsche or the German romantic philosophers. Obviously the source of our troubles is not so easily localized, and these works, despite their good intentions, are simply learned party-pamphlets. We need, on the contrary, a treatment of Nietzsche such as Professor George Allen Morgan has produced, bringing us from the past neither an echo nor a protest, but the results of sober reconnoitering. In this light it is easy to imagine a work on Egyptian civilization which would be relevant to our day and a work on Cromwell which would not.

These two negative commandments seem to me to form the common ground of contemporary historical philosophy, regardless of schools and individual tech-

[9] An excellent discussion of the faults here summarized in two sentences is to be found in Robert Livingston Schuyler's article, "The Usefulness of Useless History," *Political Science Quarterly*, March 1941.

niques. History does not yield scientific laws and its present usefulness is not fulfilled by reading back our prejudices into the past. The second part of the historian's philosophy amounts, like every other craft, to a compromise among difficulties. Some feel that the traditional demands of the Ranke-Freeman school still suffice. Verification and Accumulation are its ideals, mixed with more or less contempt for imagination and literary skill.[10] And it has indeed erected monuments that command our undiminished admiration. Others, with whom I agree, believe that the time has come for condensing and giving shape to the heaped-up materials. Consequently the historical virtues become, in ascending order of value: accuracy, intellectual honesty, and artistic imagination. I have implied these three criteria in my review of the historical forms, which I may summarize here for the sake of illustrating the working of the criteria. Schoolbooks are defective because they neglect everything but conventional accuracy. They speak in a dead language of things that never were on sea or land. The journalistic arts suffer from a kindred standardization and merely repeat their cliches with a view to satisfying the sentimentality of the public. A good part of scholarship, being either clumsy in its expression or indifferent to its effect, does

[10] Every student of history should give himself the pleasure of reading Frederic Harrison's lively dialogue contrasting the Freeman and the modern view: "The History Schools," 1893, reprinted in *The Meaning of History*, N.Y., 1902, pp. 118-138. In practice, Freeman himself paid considerable attention to prose style and Ranke is perhaps the most readable of German historians.

nothing to train the reader's mind to see, feel, or grasp the foregone reality. Just as there are people who recount the detail of their toilette with as much unction as their sorrows or their loves, so there are historians who can speak of a famine as if it were a royal wedding. To them "a fact is a fact is a fact." Lastly, the average popularizer, when he fails, does so through lack of perspective on his public and on his materials, the resulting work being either repellent or feeble.

But, it may be asked, what in all this has become of historical truth? May it not be isolated and found like a nugget even at the bottom of shallow and muddy streams? I need not speak here of the relative truth of history, I need only apply to the uses of the lay reader what I have said about the general nature of history. What he may legitimately ask from history is to be given correct information in three dimensions. If he is sensitive and persevering, he will develop what we mean by the historical sense. Readers of Henry James will remember how in the unfinished novel, *The Sense of the Past*, the hero gradually discovers that he is living not only in 1910 but also in 1820. But with a sure instinct, the novelist makes it clear that his hero is constantly aware of both his incarnations. It is not the old fiction of a passing dream, it is a simultaneous reality, and the people of the earlier date are equally alive to the stranger's similarity and difference to themselves. This happy invention deserves to symbolize the growth and maturing of the historical sense. Its substance is a strong conviction that we possess a portion of history. Often we get a fallacious sense that we are in possession. Mr. Lytton Strachey did much to make us feel that we had the Victorians in the hollow of our hands. That was a mistake which a more experienced historical tact would have avoided. For the great enemy of the historical sense is not error but convention, and it is useless to break down one convention only to replace it by another equally narrow. If all the Victorians look alike in the guise of grotesque humbugs, we have gained little over the former gallery of stiff-bosomed saints.[11] The antidote to conventionality is not debunking, but variety, which is a test the lay reader can always apply. He must hold steadfast to the knowledge that the events and persons of history were each unique, individual, induplicable, different from us; and yet that all history is human history, that is to say, intelligible, communicable within broad limits, popular in the ideal sense of the word.

To obtain histories that fulfill these requirements we must obviously have not one historian or school but many, with as many different styles, limitations, and powers. They remain of one kind only insofar as they consider history an applied art. In the works of the successful masters—Herodotus, Gibbon, Macaulay, Michelet,[12] Mommsen—it is evident that a special pas-

[11] On the problem of the Victorians, see G. M. Young's review of Wingfield-Stratford's *Victorian Sunset*, *Life and Letters*, Vol. VI, No. 33, February 1931.

[12] For the point at which Michelet deviated from his true path as an historian, see Gooch, *History and Historians in the Nineteenth Century*, and my article "Romantic Historiography as a Political Force in France," *Journal of the History of Ideas*, June 1941.

sion animates the hand. They desire to be read and hence they keep their lay audience in view; they condense, polish, construct. They desire to affect the present and hence by a sort of shuttling action they give form to the tradition they are studying, and which a moment since was merely chronicles or archives. They desire to understand and hence, within the limits of human fallibility, their virtue is fastidious: they do not suppress or add or falsify. They aspire to fame as *historians* and hence they respect the narrative form which is neither sermon, novel, essay, nor dialogue. These four desires, when coordinated, enable them to select, to keep proportion, and to achieve an atmosphere of spiritual balance which communicates itself directly to the reader. In their hands History is communication, is truly popular.

THE SCIENCE OF HISTORY

By HAJO HOLBORN

The Science of History

THERE has been much complaint of the slight interest that the public, even the educated public, has shown in historical research. The students of history look with some envy at the natural sciences which enjoy general public acclaim because of their obvious usefulness to society. The natural sciences offer definite results and valid truths. The whole organization of our daily life proves the gigantic progress that the human mind has made in mastering nature. High hopes have been entertained that the expansion of the natural sciences would ultimately place the well-being of the human race on a safe and objective basis. These expectations have been cruelly shattered by the experiences of the last years. Technology does not merely improve the efficiency of peacetime organization, but of war organization as well. The gruesome story of the destruction wrought by modern arms is as much a result of the progress of natural sciences as the millions of jobs created by their inventiveness.

It would be as serious a mistake to blame the terrors of our age upon the natural sciences as it was to expect from them the solution of the issues which have been and will forever remain human and moral problems. The natural sciences are dealing with means and not with ends. They have in fact made one great contribution to general education. They have freed man from superstitious beliefs in nature. By demonstrating that the process of nature can be explained by laws of reason they have given courage to all those who endeavor to expand the power of the human mind into all fields of life. But a concrete program of social and individual life is beyond the realm of the natural sciences.

If we turn our attention to the part played by historical thought in modern history we may feel even more disappointed. A philosopher recently asked whether the battle raging in Russia—the greatest battle in history in terms of number of men and extension of battlefield —was not actually a conflict between the left and right wing of Hegel's school. Without doubt ideological wars are to a very large extent traceable to diversions of historical thought which thus acts as a destructive rather than liberating force. In the growth of modern nationalism the influence of the teaching of history is of primary significance and has done much to foment the bellicose instincts of men.

But the critical historian will say that this is not history, but human passions, myth and interests costuming themselves in historical dress. He will maintain that at least the science of history is above the heat of battle. This does not mean that he himself as an individual has entered a realm of calm objectivity. But he trusts that the ideal of a science of history can be made evident by a common effort of scholars, and that the science of history is one of the strongest forces in the defense of civilization as such. Moreover, he would state his belief that critical historical research has produced results which are as valid and useful as the conclusions of natural sciences. This is the point of view we are taking when we talk of a science of history. Great confusion surrounds the term. Different people have understood it differently. They have postulated full identity of method in natural and historical studies. History is supposed to yield laws by which the whole historical process can be classified. But such a definition of the science of history is nothing but a reflection of the exaggerated significance which was at times assigned to the natural sciences outside their own field. To talk about a science of history means nothing but an affirmation of the critical and systematic approach to history, and the validity of the results achieved in this way.

To understand the science of history we are well advised if we turn to those who created it and brought it to highest perfection. Two men seem to me to tower above all other historians: Thucydides and Ranke. The first of these was an active statesman and soldier who had to live through the greatest catastrophe that imagination could conceive. The second, a scholar and teacher by profession, was born amidst the turmoil of the World War that followed in the wake of the French Revolution. In contrast to Thucydides, Ranke saw the pattern of the old Europe emerge again, if considerably modified, and the continuity of historical development restored. Both represent the greatest progress made in their age toward a critical study of history, and modern historical research and writing still rest on the foundations which they have laid.

Certain ideas or images of past and future constitute a basic element of any civilization, and all of them show a certain historical consciousness. But, of the twenty-odd civilizations which we know, only a few have given historical thought the prominent place in life that it assumed in the Ancient World and its affiliated civilization, the Western World. Historical thought has been one of the mainsprings of action and contemplation in the history of western man. Moreover, only in ancient and western civilization did historical consciousness grow beyond the primitive stage of mythological interpretation, or even beyond the next two stages of the human interest story on one side, and the factual state chronicle on the other. These three types of history writing we can find in a good many civilizations. We meet them in the Old Testament where mythological interpretation appears side by side with the chronicles of kings and the novelistic treatment of episodes of the past in the stories of David, Absalom, etc. The same forms of historical writing can be found in other civilizations, in the first place in Greece. The Greeks, however, went one step further by trying to replace the mythological and poetic by a scientific interpretation of history. At the same time when, in Ionian civilization, the science of nature superseded the old cosmology, the memorable attempt was made to explain history without reference to the miraculous and legendary, and to find its explanation in the immanent qualities of human life. It was Thucydides who defined the task of the new history.

"On the one hand I have given no greater credence to the accounts turned into song by poets adorning and amplifying their theme than I have on the other hand to the chroniclers who composed with a view rather of pleasing the ear than of telling the truth, since their stories cannot be tested, and most of them have from lapse of time so won their way into the region of the fabulous as to be incredible. . . . As to the facts of the occurrences of the war, I have thought it my duty to give them, not as ascertained from any chance informant nor as seemed to me probable, but only after investigating with the greatest possible accuracy each detail. . . . And it may well be that the absence of the fabulous from my narrative will seem less pleasing to the ear; but whoever shall wish to have a clear view both of the events which have happened and of those which will some day, in all human probability, happen again in the same or a similar way—for these to adjudge my history useful will be enough for me. And, indeed, it has been composed, not as a prize-essay to be heard for the moment, but as a possession for all time."

The twenty-second chapter of Thucydides from which this quotation has been chosen was the first program of a science of history. The legendary and fabulous were banned from the realm of historical study, and accurate truth, achieved by critical analysis of contemporary sources, became the exclusive aim of historical research. Rhetorical or literary brilliance for its own sake was also excluded, but "usefulness" in a philosophical sense was proclaimed the highest criterion. When Thucydides proudly stated that his work was designed as an "everlasting possession" he wished to express his belief that it enshrined truth as objectively valid and useful as the results of any other branch of science.

Critical methods for the gathering of historical evidence did not in themselves raise historical studies to the rank of a science. Otherwise Thucydides would have written annals or a series of important incidents of the Peloponnesian War. But to Thucydides the truthful reconstruction of the past was the means for opening up a view on the general causes and motives of human action. Thucydides expresses this ultimate goal of his history by using a literary device which modern historians could not imitate. In his work the protagonists of the historical drama give speeches reflecting on the profound issues of the war. He has been harshly criticized by modern scholars for inserting idealized or fictitious speeches. But since he himself states that these speeches were not authentic in the literal sense, he could hardly be accused of forgery. A careful study of the speeches would show that they contain a great element of realistic truth, and beyond that reflections which are not essentially different from the observations that a modern writer would add to his descriptive narrative. Modern historians were tutored in literary expression by the prose writers of the eighteenth and nineteenth centuries, Thucydides by the Athenian poets and sophists. He was, therefore, likely to personify the different aspects of the truth, as in the Greek dialogue, or as in the comments of the chorus in the Athenian tragedy where the light of the truth is broken into its component colors by a number of persons presenting different views.

The deeper meaning of Thucydides' speeches becomes evident in an examination of their place in the work as a whole. The touch of genius appears in the device by which Athens is first characterized by its enemies. From the speech of the Corinthian minister in Sparta the reader learns for the first time how the neighbors of Athens felt the pressure of her might and the threat of her political cunning. But through accusations and detractions the reader begins at the same time to realize some of the greatness of the Athenian commonwealth. In subsequent chapters new glimpses are afforded, culminating in the funeral speech of Pericles in which the essence of Athenian democracy is fully illuminated.

Such methods were in line with the literary taste of the age, but Thucydides did not use them for mere adornment. Even in this respect his aim was not the beautiful, but the useful or, as we may say now, science rather than literature. The underlying issues of the war are characterized from different angles and so thrown into full relief. The pattern of human life, as the philosophical mind of Thucydides sees it, becomes apparent through the deliberate use of these various perspectives, and for this reason the speeches are essential means to express the historian's intent. To the son of the Greek *polis* man is a political being and history is accordingly political history. The currency in which the great changes of history are registered is power and force. The Peloponnesian War was inevitable with the growth of Athenian might in which the other Greek states were bound to find a vital danger to their own freedom. Moral guilt has no meaning in judging historical catastrophes, since they occur by force of nature.

There exists, however, for Thucydides another level of human life. In treating the decisive turning point of the war, the failure of the Sicilian expedition, he indicates that the strategy of the conquest of Sicily was sound. The plan miscarried because of the fall of Alcibiades. When he was banned from Athens the only statesman who could have directed the execution of the scheme with hope of success was expelled from active leadership. Thucydides does not doubt that Alcibiades invited violent criticism by his personal conduct. The intellectual qualities of a political leader were coupled with frivolous passions. Thus he unsettled the balance of forces on which the Athenian state had rested. Passions were the motives of human action, but they could be moderated and led into the right direction by reason and wisdom. Athens had achieved such leadership in figures like Pericles. A similar equipoise had existed in communal life as well. Athenian government, culture, arts and sciences were the result of a high vitality tempered by wisdom. But in Alcibiades private passions and public virtues were in conflict, and consequently the passions of the mass could triumph over prudent leadership. His fall was the prologue to the rule of the demagogue.

Moral forces play a part in human history insofar as the education of a nation and its leadership determine policies. This interpretation shows Thucydides as a student of contemporary Greek philosophy and science. His concept of man, his ideas about passion and reason bear the impress of the scientific speculation of his day. From here stems what is usually called his "objectivity." In his treatment he takes a standpoint far above the struggling factions of the day. He finds an explanation of causes, motives, and results by relating them to what he conceives to be the profoundest conception of human life. This enables him to lend life and color to friend and enemy alike. His own role during the war becomes incidental, just a welcome opportunity to gather material and to gain a more realistic understanding of the events of the war. The historian has forgotten his earthly station by ascending to the heights of humanity to which Greek philosophy and education had opened a path.

There is an individual pride in Thucydides, which was closely connected with another idea of his history. In the funeral speech of Pericles Athenian civilization is described as the highest form of culture to which the Greeks had risen. For Thucydides its ideals were not invalidated by the political catastrophe of 404 B.C. He had seen them lowered by the Athenians themselves and later brought down by their enemies, but his faith that no higher human achievement existed, that they were also "useful" for all time, was not shaken. In the Athenian philosophy he found the most logical system of explanation of human life. By adapting it to history and illuminating the tragic cataclysm of the Peloponnesian War he wanted to testify to the everlasting quality of the scientific mind.

The critical analysis of sources and the reconstruction of individual scenes of the past was to Thucydides but a *methodos* and this means a way to something. As a doctor would be unable to determine the state of health without a careful examination of the symptoms of a disease, thus the diagnostician of historical life has first to verify the phenomena in which this life demonstrates its reality. But the goal of the study of history is to understand past events and conditions as the logical outcome of human nature and of its place in the world. As far as an historian is unable to transcend the limitations of his own private experiences he is inclined to identify human nature with his own self. Critical participation in the general knowledge of a civilization provides him with guiding stars for a more than subjective understanding of history. The wealth of the scientific and philosophical ideas of Ionia and Athens contributed to the range of Thucydides' vision. In choosing his position in the intellectual discussion of his age he was enabled to proceed from the actual events to the human sources of action.

This was the beginning of the science of history and for two thousand years the critical approach of Thucydides was not matched by any historian. This does not mean that there were no other great historians; in fact, even some of his predecessors could be placed above him in certain respects. Herodotus surpassed him in his interest in universal history, which, after two centuries, was revived by Polybius to become later the basis of all Christian historiography. Herodotus was not only more universal, but also more catholic in his studies. In contrast to the political history of Thucydides, monographically written, Herodotus's history is of universal scope, and deals with folklore, culture, and religion as well as politics. But Herodotus was not able to avoid the pitfalls of such universal curiosity. The logical unity of his work suffered.

In turning from Thucydides to Leopold Ranke we should again not forget his precursors. The old commonplace statement that the eighteenth century was unhistorical has long been discarded. The eighteenth century was one of the greatest centuries of historical thought. Nor did progress cease with Ranke. But there can be no doubt that in him historical consciousness reached a new height of maturity, and that in the enormous range of his works and teaching no modern historian has equalled him. He himself stated: "We have great teachers not in order to stick to their words and to repeat them; it is only the spirit who vivifies in science as elsewhere."[1] This spirit wrestled with the fundamental problems of the science of history during a long life.

From his ninetieth year the following remark of Ranke on the origins of his first work has come to us: "In the twenties of the nineteenth century the conviction spread that only a deeper study of the foundations of states and empires would satisfy the needs of the future. The romantic historical writings of Walter Scott . . . contributed chiefly to awaken an interest in the actions and attitudes of past ages. I was myself sufficiently attracted by them and I read more than one of these works with lively interest, but I was also offended by them. Among other things I was hurt by the way in

[1] *Collected Works*, Vol. 51-52, p. 497.

which Charles the Bold and Louis XI were treated in his *Quentin Durward*, in full contradiction to the historical sources, even in the details. I studied Commines and the contemporary reports . . . and gained the conviction that Charles the Bold and Louis XI, as Scott depicts them had never existed. The good and learned author probably knew that himself. But I felt unable to pardon him for adding traits to his treatment which were entirely unhistorical and for presenting them as if he believed them. In comparing the two I gained the conviction that the historical reports themselves were more beautiful and, in any case, more interesting than the romantic fiction. Thereafter, I turned away from it altogether and decided to avoid everything fictitious and fanciful and to cling strictly to the facts."[2]

The parallelism with Thucydides is close, and in fact Ranke himself often confessed that he learned more from Thucydides than from any other historian. The programmatic preface with which he accompanied his first work in the year 1824 makes this influence quite clear, indicating at the same time the new direction which he gave to historical studies. His first book was entitled *Histories of the Latin and Germanic Nations, from 1494-1514*. In the introduction he explained that neither the old concept of a universal Christendom, nor that of Europe as such, nor even that of a Latin Christianity could logically be used as a framework of modern history. Only by studying the Latin and Germanic nations together could he find the unity that

[2] *ibid.*, Vol. 53-54, p. 61.

underlay all modern history. Their growth showed a common pattern and a continuous exchange of ideas affecting their lives. Their unity in peace and war seemed to Ranke the true theme of modern history, and he proposed to prove their close community by the study of their life on the eve of their greatest division, just before the Reformation.

The insistence upon the inherent unity of the subject is in principle very similar to Thucydides' demonstration of the common history of the Hellenic states and its tragic culmination in the Peloponnesian War. And again he seems partly to point back to Thucydides in the following famous remarks: "History has had assigned to it the task of judging the past, of instructing the present for the benefit of the ages to come. The present study does not assume such a high office; it only wants to show *wie es eigentlich gewesen*." The literal translation would be: "It only wants to show what actually occurred." But a more correct rendering would be: "It wants merely to reconstruct the actual past." After this statement Ranke moves even closer to Thucydides. Only contemporary sources, critically sifted and cross-examined could form the basis of research, and then he goes on to say:

"Out of the subject and the material comes the form. You could not expect from history the same free treatment of its subject which is looked for, at least in theory, in a work of literature, and I do not know if those are right who find this in the works of Greek and Roman masters. Strict presentation of the facts, conditional and unattractive though they may be, is unquestionably the

supreme law. Next seems to me to come the presentation of the unity and of the progress of events. Instead
of starting with a general description of the political
institutions of Europe, which would perhaps have confused and certainly have diverted attention, I have
preferred to describe each nation, each power, each
individual more extensively only at the time when it
assumes an active or leading part."[3]

A unified subject, critical study of sources, accuracy
of presentation, and an organization of the narrative in
which each stage appears as the logical result of the
earlier events and in which all historical forces are
strictly subordinated to the general development—these
are the chief maxims of Ranke's history. The difference between Ranke and Thucydides seems almost
negligible. But two points deserve special consideration.

What did Ranke have in mind when he declined to
act as a judge of the past? To Thucydides, as we have
seen, the moral judgment was not a genuine historical
judgment, either. Historical events were to him symptoms of growth. He comes sometimes close to an organic or biological interpretation, most clearly in the
chapters in which he describes the transformation of
the human mind under the impact of the war in terms
of a medical history or a feverish illness. Thucydides
underlines this viewpoint by turning immediately thereafter to the history of the plague in Athens, from the
pathology of history to pure pathology. Historical
events are analyzed by him with cold anatomy. The

[3] *ibid.*, Vol. 33-34, p. vii.

ideal values are far above the sufferings of mortal men, no ray from the stars is able to melt the heart of the goddess of fate, *Tyche*, who holds men bound by her austere laws.

Ranke's Christian consciousness made such an interpretation impossible. Christian religion had brought heaven and earth closer together. The individual was able to overcome *Tyche* and to experience the reality of metaphysical and moral values in his own life. Whether or not such an approach was logically bound to result in a theology of history is doubtful; in any event it made it impossible to look at individuals merely as fodder for the mills of historical fate, or at best as types and symbols of groups and ages. Obviously the individual was now to be judged in terms of both his actions and his intentions as well, how far he achieved Christian perfection. The same applied to generations and periods.

Ranke did not question the Christian attitude. He never entertained any doubt that the individual had a destiny apart from his participation in the historical process. Moreover, he knew that moral and ideal forces had a direct bearing on the course of historical events and that the struggle between them and the stubborn reality of matter took place in the life of the individual. He was, therefore, tremendously interested in biography and fathered the idea of a German National Biography (*Allgemeine Deutsche Biographie*), a work which served as a model for similar undertakings in other countries. But he considered biography as a mere auxiliary branch of historical science. He himself wrote no true biography. His monograph on Wallenstein he called a *History* of Wallenstein, his book on Hardenberg, "Hardenberg and the History of the Prussian State." There are two small biographical articles in the fifty-four volumes of his collected works, both of them in annexes to other writings, and both of them dealing with what he considered pathological cases, namely the two "digressions" on Don Carlos and on Queen Christina. As a rule the individual appears in Ranke's histories at such moments when he appears in "an active or leading role" of general history. In each case Ranke takes great pains to delineate the individual carefully and to determine his original contribution to the event, but he refuses to act as a moral judge.

As far as we can see Ranke's treatment of the individual was motivated by various considerations. The first was chiefly critical. The historian, he said, sees into the face of persons of the past, but he is unable to see into their hearts. He felt that the depth of personal life was unfathomable by critical reason and reached into a realm that preceded and transcended history. From this Ranke concluded that the individual was a legitimate subject of study only as far as his impact on the course of general history could be verified and known. With these assumptions it would be illogical to assign to history the task of passing moral judgment upon individuals. The historian has to understand and record, as Ranke once put it, "the origins and forms of all the actions and sufferings of this creature, at the same time wild, fierce, and reckless, and good, noble, and calm, of this contaminated and pure being, which we are ourselves."[4] But the historian has to understand these actions as manifestations of human nature as it unfolds in the world of time.

Here a second line of thought becomes visible, and this is the one which leads farthest beyond Thucydides. Thucydides believed in the unalterable character of man. By a monographic treatment of history he felt certain that he could grasp the meaning of human actions, not merely in the period under review, but for all time to come. What some modern historians consider to be the very essence of historicity, namely the notion of the uniqueness of all forms of historical life, was entirely lacking in Thucydides. Ranke's emphasis upon the uniqueness of the individual or of an individual period of history has profoundly influenced such a definition. Meinecke's great work on the origins of modern *Historismus* seems to me to suffer somewhat from this narrow definition of historicity.

When Ranke refused "to instruct the present for the benefit of ages to come" and reduced his study "to the reconstruction of the actual past" he took issue, of course, with Thucydides' pragmatic view of history. To Ranke there was no repetition in history, either in individuals, or in situations and ages. Therefore no recurrence of the past was to be expected in the future. This would have confined the task of reconstructing the past to a visual operation. "History wants merely to see and to understand in order to report what it sees," we read in the introduction to Ranke's second book on

[4] *ibid.*, Vol. 53-54, p. 162.

The Serbian Revolution of 1829, a book that Niebuhr called the greatest book on contemporary history which he knew. But Ranke's general attitude to history and politics is not adequately described in such statements. They were largely polemic remarks made against that type of philosophy of history which was represented by Voltaire and the Enlightenment, and had found a modified expression in Hegel's teachings. These philosophies of history postulated a predetermined goal of history and maintained that all individual events were only illustrations of one and the same scheme of historical evolution.

Ranke's and his successors' objections against this type of philosophy of history has unfortunately induced historians and philosophers to assume a logical incompatibility of philosophy and history altogether, an entirely arbitrary exaggeration most harmful to the growth of our studies. Ranke restored the critical method of historical research so much neglected, or even disregarded, by the philosophers of history of the Voltaire and Hegel school. In this he was clearly influenced by the model of natural sciences and their inductive method. But this was not yet history to him. History was not merely to be visualized, but to be understood, and it could be understood only in reference to the totality of the historical process.

In connection with the discussion of the problem of historical versus biographical treatment we have already noticed Ranke's anxiety to secure unity in his study of an historical subject, and we have seen that he found this unity in the "progress of events." He conceived of history as a unified process, not as a conglomeration of various fields of study to be cultivated by the same method. The monographic approach was to him only a preparation to universal history. Although he resented the attempts of certain philosophers to formulate a priori laws of universal history, the conception of a universal history itself was in his mind from his early days and gained clearer shape as his studies progressed. He saw individual forces in history everywhere, but he recognized in them the manifestion of a general ideal power. There is no history, but only the life of animals, as long as the mind is not accentuating human actions and producing individual forms of life. This interaction between the mind and nature is the universal principle to be used by the historian. The concept of uniqueness found its counterpart in that of universality.

In one of the last volumes of his Universal History written shortly before his death he described his position in this manner: "Apart from and beyond the histories of individual nations I assume a specific principle of universal history: it is the principle of a common life of the human race which dominates the nations without resolving itself in them. One could call it culture, preservation and expansion of civilization, not of culture alone, as it is usually understood, which would narrow down the horizon to sciences and arts. Civilization comprises at the same time religion and state, the free development of all these forces looking toward the ideal. Civilization forms the foremost acquisition and possession of humanity handed on and augmented from generation to generation . . . it is inseparably bound together with politics and war and with all the events which constitute the facts of history. The idea of universal history does not appear in generally valid forms, but in a variety of forms according to the special life of the nations and not at all in peaceful and undisturbed development but the continuous conflict and struggle; for to quarrel is the nature of man."

This was the answer of the mature scholar Ranke. History had become to him, instead of the critical and optical exploration of isolated subjects, the critically enlightened awareness of human civilization in its totality. Thucydides could not have stated the task of the historian in this form. Ranke, by summarizing experiences of the Christian era, was in fact the fulfillment of Herodotus as well as of Thucydides, giving to historical studies the broadest vision and the power to implement that vision at a moment when the history of western civilization became world history.

The reason for recalling the two greatest historical writers has been to show the birth of historical science. We should not dogmatize on their work. I have left out aspects of Ranke's work which were less of an achievement. It should be admitted that his abstention from judgments was not always the result of a higher wisdom but a desire to avoid controversial topics. His own political views deserve less criticism than they have usually found. Very few of his works are really marred by such biases, and in some of his writings on contemporary history he has shown an insight which should still make them preferred reading for modern students of history. But it is probably correct to say that the experience of the restoration of the old powers and ideas after the revolutionary and Napoleonic wars made him exaggerate the continuity and even the validity of the old forces. At times he went so far as to become an advocate of the political *status quo*, presenting his views as a result of historical research. The statesman-scholar Thucydides, under the impression of defeat, did not mix with the politics of his day; the professor was not to the same degree shaken out of his personal aspirations.

But all these questions are of minor significance for our problem. No individual could ever hope to identify his own position with the idea of science itself. This, however, does not prove science to be an illusion. We have seen the intellectual experiences which set Thucydides and Ranke on the road to historical truth. Both chose the critical method so closely akin to the natural sciences, or to Hippocrates in one case and to Descartes in the other. But the critical method by itself would not have made them historians. Their concept of history was the result of a general examination of the objective results of their own civilization, and this meant a critical participation in the discussion of human nature. The concept of history and the philosophical concept of man are inseparably bound together, and no scientific history is possible without the free study of both these problems. Wherever the concept of man is merely the reflection of human passion, the science of history ceases to exist.

It is on this level that philosophy and history come

together. They are joined together by their common effort to understand man. History describes him in his concrete variety and unity in time. To do it critically and scientifically, the student of history has to overcome the subjectivity of his initial position. This implies a reorientation and self-analysis which can find its direction only by an active participation in the fundamental intellectual efforts of the age. For history is the critical consciousness of civilization about its own past. As such, it can claim a decisive part in general education, but it can maintain its critical vigor only by preserving its universal outlook in exchange with other branches of knowledge. Our historical studies would become saltless if they ceased to feel themselves in the midst of the Humanities. The significant function of history is to remind men of the role of human nature in time and history through a progressive understanding of the processes of human civilization. This perspective is at the same time a moral postulate: to maintain the dignity of man and his heritage of civilization.

BIBLIOGRAPHICAL NOTE

The books of Friedrich Meinecke have given a fresh stimulus to the study of Ranke. From his *Weltbürgertum und National-staat* (1908), to his *Die Idee der Staatsräson* (1924) and to his latest work *Die Entstehung des Historismus* (1936) he has remained both the outstanding student and interpreter of Ranke. Among more recent studies of Ranke, G. Masur, *Rankes Begriff der Weltgeschichte* (1926) and H. Simon, *Ranke and Hegel* (1928) deserve special attention.

Recent research has opened a new understanding of Thucydides. Apart from H. Schadewaldt's challenging monograph, *Die Geschichtsschreibung des Thucydides* (1929), and the admirable article by J. Finley, Jr. "The Unity of Thucydides' History" (*Athenian Studies presented to William Scott Ferguson*, 1940), the author feels a strong obligation to O. Regenbogen's article on Thucydides in *Das humanistische Gymnasium*, Vol. 43 (1933) and to the classic chapter in W. Jaeger's *Paideia* (1934, English translation 1939). At the time when this article had gone to press J. Finley published his *Thucydides* (1942).

THE ECONOMIC IMPACT ON HISTORY

By *HERBERT HEATON*

The Economic Impact on History

A HUNDRED years ago last spring the University of Jena conferred the degree of Ph.D. on the twenty-three-year-old author of a thesis entitled "The Materialistic Philosophy of Epicurus and its Theological Criticism by Plutarch." The new doctor had not found that college days are the happiest years of one's life. He had failed to shine as a freshman at Bonn, had done little better at Berlin, had drifted back to Bonn, and finally took his degree at Jena. Girl trouble, money trouble, emotional and intellectual disturbances, all had thwarted his progress. His advisers—not official ones, but young instructors—had nagged him to "get that thesis written," and had reminded him that a doctor's degree was an essential prerequisite to an academic career. Yet just when that career seemed to be within grasp, he and they found that their radicalism was unacceptable to the new Minister of Education. Hence our hero had to abandon the dream of a life in a professor's chair; by way of compensation, or frustration, he took on the role of journalist, editor, columnist, pamphleteer, writer of manifestoes, economist, philosopher, sociologist, cultural anthropologist, and revolutionary. In that career he lit candles—or rather forest fires—which have not yet been put out.

Herr Doktor was—as you may have guessed—Karl Henry Marx. I need not apologize for introducing his name in a time which has seen the *Communist Mani-*

festo of 1848 accepted by a federal judge in Minneapolis as evidence against twenty-eight men accused of sedition. But in any year Marx would be the natural starting point for a discussion of the economic impact on history. For it was he, and his right-hand man, Engels, who first forcefully enunciated the thesis that economic conditions and trends are the explanation and driving force in the story of mankind.

Since my colleagues in this series are dipping at least their toes into the stream of historiography, may I do the same for a few minutes, and consider how Marx reached his revolutionary interpretation of history. Philosophically he was a child of Hegel, but had what we might call a father complex. Like the rest of the young radicals in his group, he accepted two of Hegel's chief theses, but disagreed violently with the third. In the first place, there was nothing wrong with Hegel's belief in growth, change, development, progress, evolution, if I may use the last two words rather loosely. In the second place, Hegel was right when he contended that progress in human affairs, like progress in the search for truth, came through the dialectic method of rebutting one argument with another, of seeing one line of development reach a certain point, then be challenged and pushed aside by an opposite one, which in turn was elbowed out of the way by a third; and so on, zig-zag, toward a less imperfect, yet never fully perfect world. But, in the third place, Hegel was all wrong when he tried to answer the question "What makes mankind move along its dialectic path, what is the driving and guiding force?" His answer was foggy and fantastic; it sounded like "the Idea," "the Absolute Idea," all-pervading and eternal "Reason," or even like "God." The world was "the external phenomenal form of the Idea," and history was the outward and visible manifestation of that Idea at work, in motion.

Since Hegel had been dead for a decade, he could not defend himself against what may have been misrepresentation. Worse still, he could not protect himself from what the young men determined to do to him, namely, to turn him upside down. For Marx and Engels soon decided that Hegel had stood dialectic on its head, and that "it must be stood right side up again if you would discover the rational kernel within the mystical shell." The metaphor, like many others used by Marx, seems mixed; there is no right or wrong way up for cracking nuts; but the meaning is clear enough for our purpose. Hegel had got his philosophy or interpretation of history the wrong way up, the wrong way round. He had mistaken cause for effect, shadow for substance.

Hegel was not the first to try to formulate a philosophy of history. Most historians of his period may still have regarded themselves as glorified chroniclers and almanac-makers, whose task was to produce authentic lists and accounts of political, military, or diplomatic events. But one or two of them, along with philosophers in general, were of the belief that there must be some guiding thread. There had been suggestions—or more—that the human story could be explained in terms of God vs. Devil, alias Whig vs. Tory or some such conflict, of chosen people, of the spirit of the race or of the age, of the play of political philosophies, of the influence of some great man or of some wicked woman. Against these psychic or psychopathic interpretations could already be placed a few partly physical explanations, such as the influence of geography, soil, or climate; but in the early 'forties none of these latter had gained much favor. Most of the explanations could therefore be classed with Hegel's as idealistic rather than materialistic, and as such they all seemed wrong to Marx. They mistook the reflection for the reality. The ideal was nothing more than the material world reflected by the human mind and translated into forms of thought. And since history recorded changes in political, social, and intellectual life, the reason for these changes would be found in material conditions, which meant in practice economic conditions.

Thus Marx and Engels found their key to unlock the doors of history, sociology, political science, and prophecy. It was indeed a master key. By 1844 Marx had decided that "Legal systems and political forms cannot be conceived as autonomous phenomena, nor as manifestations of the so-called general unfolding of the human spirit. They are rather rooted in the material conditions of life which Hegel, after the fashion of the English and French of the eighteenth century, summed up under the name civic society. The anatomy of this civic society is to be found in its economics." This conclusion was elaborated, expanded, and enunciated on many occasions during the next four decades. It was implicit in almost every paragraph of the Communist Manifesto, and explicit in such sentences as that which declared that "The executive of the modern State is but a committee for managing the common affairs of the whole bourgeoisie." During the rest of his life Marx took the theory for granted, and only occasionally expounded and referred to it. But Engels seems to have kept it nearer the front of his mind, and in 1888, five years after Marx's death, he reiterated it in its most concise and extreme form. "In every historical epoch," he declared, "the prevailing mode of economic production and exchange, and the social organization necessarily following from it, form the basis upon which is built up, and from which alone can be explained, the political and intellectual history of that epoch."

In this statement Engels provides us with an X-ray photograph of any "historical epoch." The skeleton shown on the plate is the "prevailing mode of economic production and exchange." He then goes on to make an historical movie. Change the mode of production and exchange; let the change go far enough to make the new mode a serious challenger of the old; then the old social organization, political forms, property relations, distribution of power, and intellectual climate must also change. The process may be more or less rapid, and in the political, religious, and intellectual fields the resistance of the *ancien régime* may be so stubborn that a violent revolution is necessary to clinch the victory of the new order. That is the way the world has always wagged. "The final causes of all social changes and political revolutions are to be sought, not in men's brains, not in man's better insight into eternal truth and justice, but in changes in the modes of production and exchange. They are to be sought not in the philosophy, but in the economics of each particular epoch."

Having explained what shapes society and what changes the shape, two other questions remained to be answered. What was the actual mechanics of change? And since the past was so simply explained, could one deduce from the present the shape of things to come? The answer to the second question was a wish fathering a forecast: the transition, already clearly discernible and inevitable, would be from capitalism to classless and therefore stateless socialism. The main value of this prediction was its reminder that there is nothing final in human institutions; consequently the main flaw in it was its assumption that socialism would be final, an economic heaven that would be eternal. To the first question the answer was the class struggle. "The history of all hitherto existing society is the history of class struggles. Freeman and slave, patrician and plebeian, lord and serf, guildmaster and journeyman, in a word, oppressor and oppressed, stood in constant opposition to one another, carried on an uninterrupted, now hidden, now open fight, a fight that each time ended, either in a revolutionary reconstruction of society at large, or in the common ruin of the contending classes." The trouble with this statement is that none of the enumerated conflicts brought about changes in the mode of production and exchange. If struggle played a part in these changes, it was conflict between landlord and merchant, between commercial capitalist and industrial capitalist, industrial capitalist and finance capitalist, finance capitalist and the SEC. The struggles between "oppressor and oppressed" were the outcome of the "social organization necessarily following from" the mode of production and exchange. They had little historical relevance to the main theme; but of course they had great propaganda value, and hence were given a prominent place in the Marxian Book of Revelations.

The Materialistic Conception of History became part of the standard equipment of Marxian socialist movements on the continent of Europe; but knowledge of it was slow in penetrating the consciousness of outsiders. In 1887 Thorold Rogers could give a course on "The Economic Interpretation of History" at Oxford and lament the neglect of "economical facts." This neglect, he said, "renders history inaccurate or at least imperfect, political economy a mere mental effort, perhaps a mischievous illusion." Yet he gives no sign of having heard of Marx. This is not, however, another example of Oxford's cultural lag, for Arnold Toynbee knew Volume I of *Capital*, in a French translation, when he gave his famous lectures on the Industrial Revolution in 1881-1882. But it was the Marxian theory of value and surplus value that absorbed his attention, as it did that of the Fabian essayists six years later, and of Alfred Marshall in his *Principles of Economics*, first published in 1890.

Then in the 'nineties the academic world suddenly discovered Marx's views on history, and the fun began. In Germany, Sombart emerged, an avowed but gently critical Marxian in his treatment of *Socialism and the Social Movement* (1896) and in his first edition of *Der moderne Kapitalismus* (1902). In Italy, Labriola,

Loria, and Croce published critical expositions. In the United States Ashley dealt with the new fad at the 1899 meeting of the American Historical Association. The new doctrine, he said, "has created so much consternation and alarm that for the last two or three years everybody who has ventured to write about economic history at all has been liable to be called upon to 'stand and deliver' his opinion as to the materialistic conception of history at a moment's notice." In 1902 Seligman gave us his careful study of the doctrine; in 1913 Charles Beard published his professedly non-Marxian *Economic Interpretation of the Constitution of the United States*; and in 1937 the American Economic Association devoted one session of its annual meeting, held at Atlantic City, to a wide-ranging examination of Marx.

Thus for about half a century social scientists, including historians, have, or should have, known the general character of the Marxian interpretation. During the same half-century a small but fairly industrious band of specialists called economic historians has been studying the story of work and workers, of Clio in overalls; mighty armies of political scientists, economists and sociologists have been watching the wheels go round or trying to discover what makes them turn; and psychologists have explored the muddy springs of human conduct. Meanwhile, Marxism, after having been modified or maltreated by central and western European socialists, has reappeared in all its original dogmatism in Russia, where it was first a road-map for Russian revolutionaries and then a syllabus for Soviet statesmen.

The results of half a century's labor are not easily
summed up, but one or two conclusions may be voiced.
The first is that economic interpretations can be whole-
hog or fractions of a hog. One can range all the way
from the admission that economic factors may play a
modest part, through all grades and degrees up to an
insistence on economic dominance or even monopolistic omnipotence. If one has an intellectual or tem-
peramental dislike of one-track minds, one can recall
that in their quieter moments Marx and Engels confessed that the heat of controversy had led them to
overstate their case, and had admitted that climate,
topography, race, custom, tradition, family relationships, religion, politics, and art react on each other as
well as on economic trends or social conditions. Even
if one goes the whole way, there are other routes than
that marked by Marx. One can assert the supreme
importance of modes of production, exchange, technology, or transportation; one can recognize the influence of classes and admit the economic and social
basis of political parties and programs; and yet one can
deny the corollaries and conclusions that Marx drew
from these premises and postulates. One can be an
economic interpretationist without being a Marxian.

The second conclusion is that academic acceptance
of the Marxist interpretation has nowhere been complete except in Russia. In that country during the last
two decades prodigious feats of valor and ingenuity
have been performed in fitting not merely broad developments but short-run events into the orthodox
strait-jacket. At least one Russian scholar has reexam-

ined the relationship between lord and serf in the medieval village. Some modern English students have lately been suggesting that this relationship was marked by at least some recognition of landlord's obligations and serf's rights; that some friction points received lubricating oil; that the custom of the manor might triumph over the will of the lord; that economic trends might strengthen the bargaining or resisting power of the serf; and that both lord and serf were human beings, not economic or social abstractions. But the communist will have none of this. The medieval village was a class battleground, the scene one of ceaseless struggle, in which the will of the lord usually triumphed over the custom of the manor and the feeble resistance of the serfs.

Another group of Russians has reinterpreted the English Civil War and the Interregnum. English and American scholars have accumulated a mountain of facts about those two devastating decades; but they have shunned simple interpretation or at best have tried to find the reason for the noise in the clash of rival religious beliefs, political philosophies, or constitutional claims. To the Russians the whole affair is childishly simple. The Civil War was a conflict of classes; it was the English bourgeois revolution. The class in possession was the old landed aristocracy, the landed church, and the landed crown. The challenging class was the bourgeoisie, which desired to break the fetters imposed by the crown's fiscal policies and the state's restrictions on industrial or commercial freedom. The bourgeoisie was allied with the progressive country gentry, who were eager to develop their own smaller estates and to lay their "improving" hands on the lands of crown, church, and aristocracy. But, strange to relate, these acquisitive traders and squires were backed by the peasants, who wished to shake off the last relics of feudalism, and by certain small manufacturing or petty trading groups who were yearning for freedom of production and trade or who resented the enjoyment by others of privileges which they did not share. When, however, the four allies had begun to defeat the common enemy, the ranks split. New party labels—presbyterian, independent, leveller—appeared, but each of them really covered an economic group or interest. When the Presbyterians, or in other words the large traders organized in monopolistic companies, had got what they wanted, they became satisfied and conservative; the revolution had gone far enough. When the Independents, alias the middle-sized industrialists and landed gentry, had gained some of their ends, they were ready to call it a day, join hands again with the big bourgeois Presbyterians, tolerate the survival of a humbled aristocracy, and defy the unsatisfied claims of the small artisans and peasants who comprised the class called Levellers. The Levellers were thus licked and tricked, and their last state was worse than their first. The aristocrats lost some of their land; some tax burdens were shifted from strong to weak shoulders; the crown was taught to behave as its economic masters wished; and a king who had grown weary of travelling was given a one-way ticket from France to London to protect aristocrat, squire, and bourgeois against a possible proletarian and peasant revolt.

Outside Russia the Marxian interpretation has found some support among young European and American scholars during the last two decades. This is not surprising, for during that period young men who have an innate urge to take sides or champion causes have had a limited range of choice. The wave of idealism of the last war gave place to one of cynicism or defeatism; and that wave was crowded with swimmers. For the rest of the new generation, the list was unattractive. Capitalism, democracy, liberalism, conservatism, orthodox labor or socialist movements, the Republican Party, the Democratic Party, all were feeble fires at which to warm one's enthusiasm for a better social order. Fascism seemed to westerners to be a counsel of sophistry and sadism. Only Communism offered a full-blooded philosophy, program, and objective to the radically-minded. Five years ago a British novelist who had been lecturing in American universities and elsewhere, asked me if I knew many Communist faculty members or students. I replied "Not many." "That's strange" the visitor remarked. "At Cambridge [England, not Massachusetts] almost everybody under fifty is a Communist." This bit of prosaic license reminded me of the assertion made by an English prince or aristocrat over forty years ago, that "We are all socialists nowadays." The accuracy of both assertions depended on definition and on the thoroughness of the survey. But at most the novelist's remark meant that some young, and some not so young, intellectuals had found satisfaction in the communist creed. At least it meant that virtually all social students knew something, and liked what they knew, about the Russian faith and works. And if they were historians by inclination or profession, they were aware that a firm of oculists named Marx, Engels, Lenin, Bukharin, and Company made spectacles which helped one to see the human story in new light, in sharper focus, and in a color that was attractive.

Recent historiography is therefore well sprinkled with studies which owe more or less of their interpretation and viewpoint consciously or unwittingly to Marx. Laski's story of the development of liberalism is probably one of the best-known. Less well-known but more ingenious was the effort made by a young English historian five years ago to settle the long controversy about the relationship between Calvinist Protestantism and Capitalism. In 1905 Max Weber, having spent part of a summer in St. Louis, thus breathing the capitalist air at its smokiest, had hazarded the suggestion that Calvinism was the distillery of that capitalistic spirit which Sombart had just declared to be the driving force of modern capitalism. The suggestion, rapidly hardening into a thesis, was grand material for a first-rate argument; and if you happened to dislike both Capitalism and Calvinism you could blame a bad cause for a worse disease. Hence for over thirty years the tide of battle swayed back and forth so fiercely that there was little time to pause and ask "If Calvinism created the capitalistic spirit, what created Calvinism?" Whether one accepted or denied Weber, everybody seemed to be agreeing that a religious change had, or had not, something to do with an economic one, and this was a nasty thought for Marxist interpreters. In 1937, therefore, one of their number, a young Briton, tried to save the situation. The controversy had troubled the world long enough; Weber had led the whole pack of historians on a false scent; the methods of inquiry used in the debate *must* lead to false results; and the only way of escape was to take a new method and a new point of departure. By so doing, it became apparent that the real sequence ran as follows: (1) the Price Revolution of the sixteenth century created opportunities for making large profits, as is always the case when a rapid rise in prices is accompanied by a slower and smaller rise in wages, and hence by a widening gap between labor costs and prices; (2) the expanding profits and the opportunities to make more of them stimulated a veritable Industrial Revolution of the sixteenth century, one which some historians claim was as significant as that of the eighteenth century; (3) these developments created new material conditions, political stresses, and social needs, which could be met only by far-reaching religious adjustments, or in other words by the Reformation. There is the sequence: Price Revolution, Industrial Revolution, Reformation; perfectly good Marx, and at least as challenging as Weber, but resting on a foundation of facts and of time-sequences that simply is not strong enough to carry the superstructure. The debate continues.

Of other European instances of the administration of strong or diluted economic determinism, there are a goodly number. Richard Pares, one of the younger

group of British imperial historians, has frankly tested
the imperialist theories of Marx, Lenin, Bukharin, and
Rosa Luxembourg against the play of economic factors
in the history of the British Empire. He reaches the
conclusion that "Not all the Marxist teachings apply
to all the facts, but many of them open the eyes of
colonial historians to things which they ought to have
seen before." Lillian Knowles, who taught economic
history in London during the first quarter of the twen-
tieth century, was at least half an economic interpretationist of the non-Marxian variety. She began the first
book she ever published with the dictum, "The nineteenth century is an outcome of the French achievement and advertisement of personal liberty combined
with the new mechanical inventions which emanated
from England. The result was the simultaneous re-
moval of legal and physical disabilities." The legal
freedom was worthless until the physical ability to
move was real. It was no good being all dressed up and
free to "go places" until improved transportation was
available to take persons and goods to the ends of the
earth. Hence she worked out what might be called a
transportation interpretation of history, which led to
such conclusions as the close relationship between the
decline in church-going and the improvements in the
ability to bring food cheaply from the far corners of the
earth. One no longer needed to pray "Give us this day
our daily bread." The tramp steamer would see to it
that the bread was available. And another outstanding
British scholar, Alfred Marshall, who was no mean
economic historian, declared in the first paragraph of

his *Principles of Economics* (First Edition, 1890) that "The history of the world has in the main been shaped by religious and economic forces," and tipped the scales in favor of the latter by deciding that "Religious motives are often more intense than economic: but their direct action seldom extends over so large a part of life."

In North America, as indeed in all parts of the New World, the economic story looms so large in the country's development that economic interpretations of political, social, legal, and intellectual history have, after a long lag, become almost normal. Purely political history or political interpretation lived long and dies hard, but it seems to be passing away at last. Turner's thesis had some economic strands, Charles Beard's had many more, and the conditions or events of the last two decades have turned many American scholars into amateur economic pathologists. Hence we have garnered a goodly crop of recent economic interpretations. Professor Louis Hacker's *Triumph of American Capitalism* (1940) is the most recent, extreme, and provocative example. It is "wholly concerned with the underlying forces, economic and political, that have made American history." But the economic underlies the political all through; Capitalism, as envisaged in the concepts and categories of Marx and Sombart, is the all-pervading ether or atmosphere, and the very title warns us of the class struggles that are to be waged between the covers of the book. While Hacker thus strives to reinterpret the general story, many regional or topical revisionists are at work. The history of Southern Reconstruction, for example, is being rewritten in terms of economic and social forces; there is less preoccupation with carpetbaggers, scalawags, and other personal devils, or with the superficial end-products of political machinery. Professor Roger Shugg has written about the origins of class struggle in Louisiana, analyzing the tussle between merchants and planters on the one hand and small farmers and laborers on the other; and it is significant that he begins, not with 1865, but with 1840. He makes no attempt to fit his story into the Marxian pattern; but some of his fellow-workers in the southern field have frankly done Marxian case studies.

If we swing from the far south to the deep north of this continent, we find some of the best interpretive work of our day being done in Canada, especially by Professor Harold Innis and his colleagues in the social science group at the University of Toronto. Canadian history was all too long centered on the romanticism of the fur trade or the dreary constitutionalities of responsible government, confederation, and dominion status. The new school starts off with a staple commodity—fur, fish, minerals, wheat, or lumber. It looks carefully at the geographical controls of rock and soil, land and water routes, climate and distance; it studies changes in the technique of production or transportation; it investigates the demand for labor, increasing quantities of capital, and more efficient organization; it examines the political consequences of the need for sinking vast sums of capital in railroads and waterways; it looks at the effects of competition or monopoly, and of changing markets or price levels on producers' demands, on political responses, and on the imperial ties that bind; and it considers the adequacy of "dated" constitutional machinery to cope with new conditions and problems. I know no other work today which rests so solidly on the rock-bottom of geography and economics, or which is so penetrating in interpretation and interrelationship as that of the Toronto School.

The economic interpretation, then, is with us. In fact, it is so much with us and has been here so long that it is already old-fashioned, and we are being urged to pass beyond it to something new and therefore vastly better. In December 1939, a mighty wooden horse was pulled into the Mayflower Hotel, Washington, D.C., where the American Historical Association was holding its annual meeting. Out of its capacious interior popped a crowd of evangelists to preach a new way to salvation, called "The Cultural Approach." Conversion apparently involved complete immersion in cultural anthropology and social psychology. Or, according to a recent communication from an American book publisher, we historians must travel the long road through Ideational, Idealistic, and Sensate Cultures; observe the subtle distinctions between the Empirical Sociocultural System and the Pure Causal and Pure Meaningful Systems; examine the Genesis, Multiplication, Mobility, and Diffusion of Sociocultural Phenomena in Space; consider critically the Metaempirical, Cosmic, Biological, and Mixed Theories of Social Rhythms and Periodicities; wrestle with the Problem of Ever-Linear, Ever-New, and Strictly Circular Sociocultural Change; note the Reason for the Super-Rhythm of Ideational-Idealistic-Sensate Phases in the Greco-Roman and Western Super-Systems of Culture; and then fall asleep in the Twilight of our Sensate Culture and Beyond. All this in four volumes—price, twenty dollars.

Middle age and Mr. Morgenthau will prevent me, I fear, from yielding to this temptation. Let me therefore be content with an attempt to estimate the effect of the discovery that economics had something to do with history. In the first place, the economic interpretation was a healthy antidote to some of the romantic, political, military, or other unilinear or surface interpretations; it was even a good antidote to the refusal to interpret at all. It gave the historian one more keyhole through which to peep; but what one sees through a keyhole depends on the size of the hole, the position of the door, and the lighting and other conditions inside the room. Even Marx could not have seen through a Yale lock. The broad relationship between the way men work, the way work is organized, and the political, religious, and intellectual patterns is so obvious that some one should have pointed it out long before Marx; and of course Aristotle did in general terms, as did others. A pastoral economy, a slave economy, or an urban industrial economy is bound to reflect in its politics, religion, and philosophy the way in which its workaday life is organized and carried on; but the mirror may be far from perfect and those who look into it may have defective vision. An urban industrial society would certainly not write its twenty-third psalm in the images and metaphors of a pastoral people. Its first sentence would not end with the word "shepherd"; but I cannot guess what word would be used instead.

In the second place, the emphasis on classes, their origin, interests, and struggles is a useful horse, provided we do not ride it too hard or assume that horse-riding is the only form of locomotion; and the identification of the ruling class or classes with certain powerful economic interests has probably helped historians more than it has hindered. In the third place, many stories and situations become much clearer when we consider the problems of producing and distributing income, of changes in costs and prices, of the relationship between the size of the "national dividend" and the amount of it appropriated by church or state, of the economic effects of war, or of the disturbances caused by short-run or long-term business fluctuations. We get fresh light on the medieval church when we regard it as a great landowner, as recipient and spender of a vast income, and as a corporate frontiersman. Feudalism looks different when we think of lords and serfs as individuals with larders to fill and regard the manorial system as a method of farm management and distribution of income. The political and constitutional problems of the sixteenth and seventeenth centuries come into clearer focus when we consider the financial needs of rulers equipped with medieval fiscal systems, in an era of rising prices, expanding range of luxury goods, and greater armament bills. Finally, the whole story of discontent, of agitation, of demands for moderate reforms or drastic change becomes more intelligible if we place it against graphs showing changes in prices or business conditions.

Thus broad movements may find at least partial explanation in the pages of economic history. In such long sweeps the lag of politics or class relations or ideas behind economic changes may eventually be overcome. Yet even here the question to be asked should not be "What was the economic cause?", but rather should be "Was the cause economic?" There has been far too much quick jumping to answer the first question rather than to consider the second. An illustration of this can be found in the popular and even academically popular explanations of much modern foreign policy, and especially of modern "imperialism." Start out with the premise that the Foreign Office, State Department, Quai d'Orsai, or whatever its name is, is the tool and servant of the capitalist class, international banker, high finance, big business, or whatever its name may be; then every imperialist move, especially of the last hundred years, is an instance of the banker or trader using the diplomat to feather his profitable nest. Unfortunately the premise breaks too often when tested; too often the story is so complex that no simple conclusion can be reached; and in an uncomfortably large number of instances one begins to suspect that it is the diplomat who is using the banker or trader as tool.

When we turn from the grand sweep of the stream of history to the ripples and rapids on its surface, the economic interpreter is in even greater danger of getting out of his depth. Try to apply the idea of class interests, or the philosophy of *laissez faire* as the guiding rule of a class, to British economic policies of the first half of the last century, and you will find you raise as many problems as you solve. The American Revolution still seems a hard nut for the economic interpreter to crack. The attitude of New England toward the Embargo and other commercial restrictions of the years 1806-1812 may be capable of explanation in terms of economic interest, though that would be far from the whole story; but the attitude of the central and southern states in welcoming and supporting a policy which ruined many of their farmers, planters, merchants, and shipowners simply does not fit into any possible picture of economic man. And the neat thesis that the War of 1812 was really precipitated by the desire of westerners to lay hands on the fat lands of Canada has been badly torpedoed. I might continue the list of insoluble cases indefinitely; but they all spring from the over-simplicity of the economic determinist's view of human motives, and from his failure to realize that politics may be more than a means to an economic end; it may be an end in itself, a paid or unpaid profession, whose practitioners may have standards of value which are not those of the ledger or rent-roll.

And so I come to the possibly surprising conclusion that economic historians are likely to be the least enthusiastic exponents, or the most stubborn sceptics of the economic interpretation of history. This scepticism does not rest on approval of the criticisms which professional philosophers have made of historical materialism. Those criticisms seem cogent to me, but I confess I do not understand a lot of the words in them. My own hesitation arises from the belief that one needs to know a lot of economic history as well as a lot of social, political, and intellectual history before one dares to start establishing relationships. Of Marx and Engels I should say what one historian usually says of another with whom he disagrees: they-were philosophers rather than historians, and their economic determinism was not the result of an extensive study of concrete history but of an *a priori* conception. When they gave the theory its shape and form, no one knew enough economic history to entitle him to be dogmatic about anything. True, there was the French Revolution just down the road, and economic changes which seemed revolutionary were taking place in northern England and other places. Yet even these two great historical movements were not completely understood at the time when they occurred, for a contemporary observer may be very superficial, partisan, and unreliable; and beyond them lay centuries about which very little was known. Hence when Engels needed an economic explanation for the Reformation he had to invent one: the bourgeoisie wanted scientific research done in order to solve some technical production problems; the Church forbade such research, and so the bourgeoisie revolted. Few facts were available about economic conditions or trends, so Engels manufactured some to fit the theory. Similarly, Thorold Rogers got many of his interpretations wrong because when data were scanty he filled in the gaps with bits of rather partisan imagination. And Arnold Toynbee, as fine a pioneer as any academic study could hope to have, unwittingly exaggerated the revolutionary character of the events which came after 1760 because little or nothing was known of conditions or trends before that date.

Thus the economic interpretation of history emerged in a period almost as rich in *histoire imaginaire* and as poor in serious studies as was the age in which the social contract theory was given prominence. It was also a period of fixed ideas concerning the character and behavior of human beings as economic types or income groups. Some of these ideas had been compounded out of the bile, bitterness, and even venom which bedevilled the social and economic controversies of the nineteenth century. Some of them were the reactions of people accustomed to wearing kid gloves when they discovered that a large part of the human race worked with bare hands and had to get them dirty. And some were the value-judgments of a sympathetic liberally-minded generation when it discovered that the early nineteenth century did not enjoy sanitary plumbing. Hence when the professional economic historian got to work, chiefly during the last quarter of the nineteenth century, he found a few facts and a host of assumptions awaiting him. Landlords, merchants, industrial employers, bankers, and workers in Lombard or Wall Street were greedy, ruthless, selfish, gross, and lolled in garish luxury. Peasants, wage-earners, and small storekeepers were, on the other hand, the embodiment of the simple homely virtues, sober, industrious, honest, but downtrodden and exploited. Rarely was this contrast of black and white questioned, and scarcely ever were the colors reversed. The villains of the play had few defendants except themselves until they belatedly began to employ public relations agents. They had been so busy doing things, and so indifferent about their reputation, that they had left the work of writing history to parsons, politicians, and professors who glorified the story of church and state but ignored or belittled that of economic enterprise, and often regarded the enterpriser as a low anti-social fellow.

Economic historians have therefore had a double task to discharge: to discover what happened, and to reexamine the story as dispassionately as possible. The double duty of discovery and revision is being discharged with as great vigor as ever today by what is now the third generation of the craft, and every decade, almost every year, sees a new story told or an old one retold. We are trying to improve the quality of the picture of economic life, to get a better and fuller idea of the way man has earned a living through the centuries. This is not always easy, for many kinds of records are scanty or do not exist. Yet new discoveries of manuscripts are made with refreshing frequency, both of public papers and of such private source materials as farmers' diaries, manufacturers' accounts, and merchants' letter books. Some of the stuff that used to be regarded as economic history is now recognized as being only the framework of policy, regulation, aid, or restraint, inside—or outside—of which men carried on their diverse enterprises; and it is the enterprise on the canvas rather than the frame that is receiving more attention. We are trying to see the farmer farming, rather than watching him go to granger meetings, embark on populist crusades, clamor for greenbacks, or lobby for more than a hundred per cent of parity. We are realizing that the history of labor is not fully or even largely told by narrating the history of labor unions or socialist movements, that the history of banking is more than an account of banking or currency laws, that trade is more than a matter of tariffs, and that even the history of business itself can be studied in terms of the accumulation of capital, the organization and administration of the enterprise, and the development of policies of production or sale. Such a shift of interest has many merits; one of them is that we get nearer to the center where work was being done and income produced, and spend less time on the grumblings, complaints, arguments, agitations, and attempts to save or achieve something economic by the exercise of political power.

This effort to improve the quality of the story is accompanied by an effort to make it more quantitative. Like most other branches of the social sciences, economic history has been infected by the virus of statistics. We want to measure movements, institutions, trends, to ask how much, how large, how fast, how representative? The subject lends itself, more than does any other branch of history, to statistical treatment, since we are dealing with material things which are usually capable of measurement. How large was the population of a period or of an area? How fast did the population grow? What was the productivity of agriculture or industry? How did prices and wages move, and how did they move in relation to each other? What was the

interest rate, and how did it change? What was happening to the national income, and how much of it
went to the state? How did landlords' rents rise or fall?
What was happening to the volume of domestic and
foreign trade during a period? How extensive and fast
were such movements as the spread of commutation of
money payments in place of servile labor services, or the
enclosure of land? How quickly did a new method,
piece of equipment, or type of organization spread over
agriculture or industry? How rapid was the "Industrial
Revolution" and what was the range of its effects?
What was the experience of profit or loss of merchants,
farmers, or manufacturers, the expectation of life of
joint stock companies, and the earning history of wage-
earners? And so on, through a long list of questions,
which formerly were not asked or were answered with
generalizations based on scanty data or on some far
from dispassionate contemporary assertion.

The achievements in this field, in spite of many gaps
in the evidence, have really been very substantial. Many
old conclusions have had to be abandoned, a sense of
proportion has been developed, and by a combination
of statistics and economic theory some new questions
have been raised, or even answered. We now have authentic price tables for most of western Europe, stretch-
ing back for at least four centuries. It is now almost
possible to draw a curve of business fluctuations back
to the sixteenth century, and a curve of long-term trends
back to the twelfth or thirteenth. British fluctuations
during the years 1790-1850 have recently been subjected to thorough scrutiny by men fully equipped with

historical, theoretical, and statistical tools. The modern period is rich enough in statistical raw material to be capable of such treatment; but even earlier centuries are not quite as poor as we used to think, and tables showing movements in wage rates, precious metal imports into Spain, exports and imports, the extent of Tudor enclosure, etc., are now available for use by those who know the fallibility of figures. Unfortunately, however, some one is sure to build on them hypotheses or theories which are far too heavy for the foundation: the list of such builders already contains some very eminent names.

Finally, the economic historian finds himself drawn, willingly or reluctantly, into the arena where social or economic controversialists are belaboring each other with value or moral judgments. Or, to put it another way, economic history is a tree in the branches of which a lot of the "popular history" as Professor Barzun calls it, has found a nest. Into one cluster of nests every high school and college student of the early nineteenth century has been forced to peep ever since the Industrial Revolution got into the textbooks. He has thus learned that a horde of wicked, or at least very energetic and greedy industrialists plunged an army of landless men, women, and children into unhealthy unsafe factories, to work for very long hours for starvation wages, and then to drag themselves off to sleep in filthy slum hovels. He knows also that governments, wedded to *laissez faire*, not merely refused to do anything to improve these conditions, but prevented the victims from organizing to protect themselves or better their lot; and that only with difficulty and time was this attitude modified under the pressure of threatening revolt, humanitarian sentiment, and new political or social theories.

The emotional reflex response to such a picture is that some bad men sinned against the light, chose evil rather than good, and created a number of new deadly sins. Faced with such burning indignation, what can the economic historian do? He can ask how far the working and living conditions were new, and discover that most of them were not. He can investigate the returns in interest and profit, to see how far a different distribution of wealth might have made substantial additions to the wages fund; and if he does this he may find that in good times industrial profits were not especially large, that they were often ploughed back into capital equipment, and that in bad times lack of profit and probability of bankruptcy were uncomfortably common. He may wonder how better houses could have been built until cheap water or drain pipes were available, until the system of local government had been revolutionized, until street transportation facilities allowed wage-earners to live at a distance from their work, until interest rates on mortgages had dropped from the high levels of the Napoleonic War days, or until medical knowledge had discovered the rudiments of public health. Or he may examine the condemnations heaped by zealous reformers or liberal historians on governments which did not do all that the reformers demanded or all that the historians, who usually side with the reformers, know was done later. He may then agree with J. H. Clapham that "There is a limit—very soon reached—to the amount of workmanlike creative legislation or administration of which any government is capable in a given time," and that "governments are perhaps entitled to be judged, not by what proved practicable in a later and more experienced day, nor by what reformers and poets dreamed and were not called upon to accomplish, but by the achievements of other governments in their own day." He may become in short a relativist, and relativity is at least as important to history as to physics or mathematics. His question must be: "What was economically, politically, or socially possible in the circumstances of the time or place, in a world where nothing is free, even 'free air,' and where men have not yet discovered how to produce abundance for all or how to be perfectly rational?" But perhaps this attitude is not easy to maintain until you pass your fortieth birthday; and it may earn for you the reputation of being the devil's advocate or the "tool of the capitalist class."

That difficulty, however, does not worry me as much as does the inability to keep in touch with the work of other kinds of historians, of economic theorists, statisticians, sociologists, and the other breeds of social scientists. Economic historians have tended to draw into their shells, to cultivate their own strip of land through the centuries, and to ignore the activities on other strips in the great "open field." Some ten years ago, when *Social Science Abstracts* was giving us a condensed account of all the articles being written by social scientists all over the world, the economic historian was surprised to discover how much useful material he could obtain from the work of geographers, anthropologists, and others; and perhaps they in turn found his work shed some light on their field of interest. Academic self-sufficiency and isolationism could not stand against that discovery; but the alternatives are as difficult in scholarship as they are in politics or political economy. It has been argued that no man who seriously tries to keep abreast of the output in his own field can have time left over to know what is happening outside it; yet the man who makes such an assertion is often a crowning refutation of his own statement. At any rate, the economic historian cannot afford to accept it. He owes too much to others, to the new viewpoints they have suggested, to the new tracks on which they have sent him exploring. A specialized but non-commercial economy is of little use to him; he must barter, and in the exchange he modestly hopes that the goods he has to offer will be attractive and durable.

NOTE

For recent discussions of trends in economic historiography, see Heaton, H., "Recent Developments in Economic History," in *American Historical Review*, Vol. XLVII, pp. 727-746, July 1942; Nussbaum, F. L., "The Economic History of Renaissance Europe," in *Journal of Modern History*, Vol. XIII, pp. 527-545, December 1941. The best guides to the work in revision and reinterpretation are the *Economic History Review*, which has been the leading journal since its foundation in 1927, and the *Journal of Economic History*, established in 1941 by the Economic History Association.

BIOGRAPHY AND HISTORY

By DUMAS MALONE

Biography and History

I F biography is not a part of history, or a close relative of history, my essay has no business being in this book. At times, however, the line of demarcation between biography and fiction, that is, historical fiction, has been so blurred that a considerable number of people have had difficulty in perceiving it. Writers of historical novels sometimes recapture the spirit of distant times more effectively than professional historians, and for some of them strong claims of historical fidelity have been rightly or wrongly made; but, whatever else may be said, their books are labeled fiction. Since a biography claims to be fact, obviously it must be judged by different standards.

It is supposed to present a fair likeness of a particular person. Yet the reader, when he picks up a biography, has no ready way of knowing in advance whether it contains a conventionalized portrait, a touched-up photograph, or a caricature drawn at the caprice of the artist. After he has read it he can pass judgment on it as a story; if it deals with a recent figure he may be able to check it to some extent on the basis of his own knowledge; and if it has to do with the more distant past he can draw upon such historical information as he may happen to possess; but, to an extraordinary degree, the authenticity of the book depends upon the intellectual integrity of the writer.

It would be absurd to say that the character, the personality, and the social background of a novelist are unimportant, for to a large extent every man writes from his own being and his own experience; but we should be more concerned about the origins of what we are supposed to trust. The responsibility of a writer of history, of course, is similar to that of a biographer, but ordinarily it is easier to test his product. There are considerably more people who are thoroughly familiar with the events of the American Revolution than there are who are well acquainted with the personal life of Patrick Henry or Samuel Adams; and often, in the case of a less eminent man, a biographer goes through personal papers which few other eyes will ever see. No one quite so easily as a biographer can falsify a record or make or mar a reputation. In any interpretation of biography, then, one must begin with the biographers.

First among them let us consider the autobiographers. Whether we start with Benevenuto Cellini or Benjamin Franklin and end with Adolf Hitler or John Buchan, we must agree that if modern men ever felt reluctant to write about themselves and their experiences, this reluctance has been progressively overcome. Any prominent person who lives long enough is now expected to produce a book of memoirs. It is easy to scoff at some of these concoctions, hastily thrown together on the basis of inexact memory and served half-baked by a stenographer, but it would be foolish to dismiss with a wave of the hand the large and important body of autobiographical literature. I suspect that it would be easier for any one of us to draw up a list of a dozen important autobiographies than of biographies;

and, after the lists have been drawn up, we might find that the former have been or promise to be the more enduring.

The man who writes about himself can draw upon personal sources which are available to no one else and can reveal motives which the most painstaking investigator might never uncover. No small part of the color which sometimes appears in works of biographical scholarship is imparted by the autobiographical fragments which they contain or upon which they draw; and in sheer interest biography may approach but can hardly hope to surpass autobiography. A man's own words are the man himself and, unless he is intrinsically dull or speaks in an antique tongue, most people prefer the sound of his voice to that of an interpreter. Fortunately, also, a necessary corrective is obvious to any but the dullest reader. One knows who the author is and forms a definite impression of his temperament, his point of view, and his trustworthiness, and judges the authenticity of his story in the light of these.

Another corrective is needed, however, and this may not be quite so obvious. All autobiographical writings must be considered in their setting of time and purpose. One would expect far more candor in a diary, like that of Pepys or William Byrd, written without thought of publication and unedited to conform with later reflections, than in a book of reminiscences, consciously or unconsciously designed to serve as an apologia. Recollections are inexact except when based on contemporary memoranda and the temptation to interpret the past in the light of what has happened since is practically irresistible. It is no reflection on Thomas Jefferson, then, to say that the Autobiography which he began at the age of seventy-seven is not entirely correct in regard to the Declaration of Independence which he penned at thirty-three. The historian would depend more on letters written in 1776 or on contemporary entries in a diary. Furthermore, while one likes to know what a man thought about his own place in history and his part in important events, one prefers to rely on the judgment of less interested parties. The self-appraisal of Adolf Hitler is hardly to be accepted as the verdict of history and the same can be said of less egotistical men than he. It is for such reasons as these that the best autobiography, while it may and often does surpass biography as literature, may and generally does take second place to the best biography as history.

Next to a man himself, the persons who know most about him are likely to be found among his contemporaries. Long ago Dr. Samuel Johnson said that nobody was qualified to write the life of a man but one who had eaten and drunk and lived in social intercourse with him. Under this definition James Boswell was admirably qualified and his *Life of Johnson* continues to be cited as the classic example of biography that was written by a contemporary who knew his subject well. Indeed, some have gone so far as to say that this is the only true biography, all that is written at a distance in time and space being pseudo-biography—a pale imitation of the real thing.[1]

[1] Wilbur L. Cross, *An Outline of Biography from Plutarch to Strachey* (New York, 1924), p. 32.

Probably this comment is only semi-serious, but there can be no doubt of the great advantages possessed by a biographer who knew his subject in intimate human intercourse, as Boswell knew Johnson and as Nicolay and Hay knew Lincoln. Anyone who has struggled with the task of reconstructing the pattern of life in a past century or even a past generation, endeavoring to discover just what sort of clothes people wore, what sort of food they ate, what sort of carriages they rode in, must realize that his handicap of ignorance is hard to overcome; and anyone who has tried to peer through external records and perceive the inwardness of things must envy the observer who was actually admitted behind the scenes. A great man may not seem great, or he may seem too great, to his valet or secretary, but what a boon to a biographer to see his subject in living action! I am sure that Albert J. Beveridge, who talked with so many people while he was writing his books, would have liked to talk with John Marshall; Douglas Freeman has followed the Army of Northern Virginia through all of its campaigns, but he must often have wished that he might have had Robert E. Lee beside him.

Biography written by a contemporary may not be the richest and truest biography, but unquestionably it can be. Pen pictures of Hitler or Mussolini or Stalin that have been drawn by present-day journalists may remain through the years the most authentic and revealing portraits that are available. Indeed, historians of the future may rely far more on first-hand journalistic accounts of the moment than upon documentary records whose very purpose may be to deceive. In this connection it may be of interest to report some observations growing out of the *Dictionary of American Biography*. Whenever we were seeking an author for the sketch of some person recently deceased we were faced with two alternatives: we could select some person who knew the subject well and run the risk of a biased interpretation; or we could select somebody who did not know him intimately, and perhaps did not know him at all, but who at least could be depended upon to view him critically. Assuming familiarity with the field in which he labored, which was the more important, personal knowledge, or what we call objective judgment? The question could not be answered categorically and doubtless we often erred on the side of impersonality and prudence. A group of scholars would be likely to do that. But, while continuing to avoid persons who were obviously biased, we became increasingly aware of the importance of choosing authors who knew more about the men they were describing than they were likely to find in print.

In judging biographical writing by contemporaries, one should certainly not condemn it because of the intimacy of information that was available to the author. It is of the first importance, however, that the exact relations of the author to the subject be known and that his bias, if any, be allowed for. A member of the family is naturally suspect. Indeed, straight autobiography is generally preferable to a family biography. No one is likely to take very seriously the biography of a politician written by a partisan or foe for use in a campaign. Perhaps political biography, more than any other, benefits from the passage of slow time and the subsidence of strife; and it is inevitable that successive generations should want to make fresh appraisals of the major heroes and villains of their nation or the world. People will continue to ask what Lincoln or Jefferson or Napoleon or Hitler mean to their age. But if we consider biography as the depiction of a man as he actually lived, there is enormous loss and wastage in long delay. Personal records are destroyed or buried almost beyond recovery in some repository, and the vividness of contemporary impressions is dulled.

The passage of time may even serve to distort perspective, for every man has a right to be judged against the background of the age in which he lived. In humanity's greatest heroes and villains there has been a timeless quality which gives them significance to later ages, and it is entirely appropriate that this be pointed out again and again. But just as figures of the past should be spared the incongruity of appearing in modern dress, so they should be viewed in their temporal setting of thought and custom. Compared with the modern physicist, Benjamin Franklin was a crude tyro, but in his own age he was a discoverer. Viewed in too long perspective, a man may lose much of the significance which was accorded him in his own generation and to which he is historically entitled.

For all of these reasons let us hope that in the future an increasing number of biographies will be written within a decade or less of the subject's death. They are unlikely to be judicious if he is still living. If a man is important enough there will be subsequent appraisals and reappraisals, interpretations and reinterpretations, but as a rule the story of a human life can be told most fully, most colorfully, and most effectively before the memory of it has grown dim.

This is not to say that the task of dealing with recent figures is an easy one. Indeed, there are problems incident to an economy of abundance which do not exist in an economy of scarcity. There are more sources of information about Abraham Lincoln and Thomas Jefferson than anyone can well take advantage of, even though these eminent men lived quite a while ago, but in general the closer one comes to the present day the more extensive his materials are likely to be and the more probable it is that he will suffer from embarrassment of riches. What mortal can ever hope to go through all the papers of Franklin D. Roosevelt or to read any considerable portion of the things that have been said about him?

The biographer of an eminent recent figure, like Woodrow Wilson or John D. Rockefeller, who has had access to private papers not available to others, may be expected to disclose some facts that were not previously known. As a rule, however, one who writes about contemporaries should be judged not so much by his success in turning up obscure documents as by the skill of his selection and by his ability to penetrate to the inwardness of things. He may not be a discoverer in the same sense as a scholar who recovers a vanished figure of long ago and whether or not we call him an historian is largely a matter of definition. He may be a journalist by profession or training and he certainly doesn't have to be an academician.

Biography is not an occult science into the mysteries of which only doctors of philosophy can penetrate. It has no complicated terminology which only specialists can understand. In the contemporary field, the materials of which it is compounded may be of easier access to a newspaperman than to a professor. In matters of literary form—as, let us say, in the choice of telling incident—the writer can learn from the better novelists lessons which are not generally taught in seminars. Even in the contemporary field, however, he cannot hope to escape the employment of methods as painstaking as those of a trained historian, and as truly as any historian he should cultivate a judicious spirit.

If he deals with an era that has closed it is hard to see how he can escape being to all practical purposes an historian. It might be assumed that biography of this sort is the special province of the professional scholar. Unquestionably he enjoys advantages here which amateurs can overcome only by long labor. Nonetheless, during the years that immediately followed the first World War, academic historians were reluctant to indulge in biography—considerably more reluctant, it may be said, than they have since become.

At that time the dicta of Carlyle and Emerson that the history of the world is but the biography of great men, and that properly there is no history, only biography, were not accepted. It would not be correct to say that professional historians were too prone to generalize, for the subjects of doctoral dissertations and of post-doctoral monographs represented a high degree of minute particularization; but certainly they were loath to individualize. They preferred to deal with groups and trends, to quote statistics, and to emphasize, not to say exaggerate, general economic factors. The candidate for the doctorate who presented a biographical subject had considerable professional obstacles to overcome. If he attempted such a subject, the chances are that he was expected to deal with it in an impersonal way; he was supposed to show an actor upon the stage, not to describe the whole of a human life. In the field of personal biography he was not a serious contender.

There were some who regarded this voluntary abnegation as fortunate. In an open letter to biographers, originally written in 1896, but not published until long afterward, Havelock Ellis bemoaned the fact that most men had come to the piano of biography from the organ of history.[2] In my opinion it would be better to speak of biography as a concerto, but the tendency of historians to drown the soloist with accompaniment is unquestionable. If I may take liberties with Havelock Ellis's metaphor, during the post-war decade a new group of performers tickled the ears of the public with new instruments, rendering old tunes in a modern tempo, while an occasional historian-biographer was playing organ music decorously in an empty church. These new performers and composers were aware of an audience which most of the scholars forgot, and the form that they followed, consciously or unconsciously,

[2] *Views and Reviews* (London, 1932), Chapter VII.

was not that of heavily annotated history but that of the novel.

This is not to say that the "new" biography, so-called, was wholly imaginary or that these writers knew nothing whatever about their subjects. Most novels require a considerable amount of observation, if not investigation, and an intimate knowledge of the scene whereon the tale is set. These writers varied, as mortals always do. As a rule, however, they were less laborious in research than a group of academic historians would have been and, presumably, they knew less about their subjects. Unquestionably they knew far more about the popular audience.

The best-known of these new performers, who made the academic gentry seem so dull and tame, was Lytton Strachey. By common consent his writings, such as *Queen Victoria*, represented the school at its best and, to a considerable degree, served as models for other writers. So far as we are concerned, the crucial consideration is the way that he and his fellows utilized their materials. To begin with, the published materials were highly selective and the treatment as a rule was brief. Judging from the success of certain novels and biographies in this country in recent years, brevity is not an absolute requisite for popularity, but most publishers and readers will agree that it helps. The emphasis was on personal life, rather than upon the public activities which the historian is prone to think of as comprising the only important part of biography—upon Victoria as a woman, not as a queen; in Maurois upon Shelley as a man, not as a poet. The solo, not the accompaniment, dominated the concerto. Furthermore, it is even easier to see now than it was a decade or so ago, when some critics mentioned it, that this was literature of disenchantment. As a rule, one was made much more aware of the frailties than of the virtues of the subject. Indeed, virtue was often made to appear pretentious, hypocritical, and unreal. Upon its face this was iconoclastic and somewhat shocking; old ladies may have shuddered, but some of them shuddered not with terror but delight. At that time iconoclasm was not really bold, for it tickled the palate of the times. Books that voice primarily the mood of the moment are unlikely to belong to the ages, except only as literature. But what emanated from Strachey's workshop was literature of a most fascinating sort. After you once picked up the book, it was hard to lay *Queen Victoria* down. It sold like a novel because it read like one, like one of the best.

When we say that a book that isn't a novel reads like one, probably the main thing we mean is that it is interesting, that it is a good tale. Not even a professor can rightly object if a biography turns out to be a corking story. One of the essentials of a good biography, indeed, is that it be a good narrative. Whether it be in the realm of action or of ideas it ought to move. If the new biographers reminded us of this, they rendered us a distinct service. No one can properly object to the choice of striking incidents and illustrations. However, it is unjust to the dead and to the living to manipulate materials to obtain effects, with the result of creating a false impression.

On this subject one should not speak categorically,

for the difficult and elusive art of biography cannot be reduced to a mechanical formula. "The truth, the whole truth, and nothing but the truth," you may say. But nobody can tell the whole truth about any important person within the limits of a book. Some exclusion is unavoidable. It is not entirely correct to say that the historical approach to biography is objective, while the fictional is subjective, for there is a degree of subjectivity in every writer and this inevitably affects his selection of materials and his judgment of them. But there are perceptible differences between men in their fair-mindedness, just as there are in their capacity for taking pains; and there are perceptible differences between writers who think first and most about fidelity to their subject and those who think first and most about interesting their audience.

Let us consider the question of sex. No one can deny that this is an immortal subject and perennially interesting to all save pre-adolescents. Without questioning the indispensability of sex in human life, one often suspects that certain novelists give a greater emphasis, or a different sort of emphasis, to it in their books than it has in the ordinary life of the average person. They do not take it for granted as something normal, but accentuate it for sociological or artistic or commercial purposes. Whether they do this or not, they may; as novelists it is their privilege.

A biographer might conceivably do the same thing, thus heightening interest while giving an entirely false impression about the subject of his book. The person whose life and character are described might be greatly surprised to read what is said about him. He might say that particular incidents upon which great stress had been laid were entirely true but that, taking his life as a whole, they were unimportant. In much the same way personal foibles may be so accentuated, to add interest to the tale, that people who knew the subject in the flesh would regard the alleged portrait as a caricature. A man may have a long nose without being a Cyrano de Bergerac. It is entirely possible for every given fact or characteristic that is mentioned in a book to be true and for the impression to be, nonetheless, wholly false. The features are all there but they are so out of proportion that the portrait is unrecognizable.

It isn't quite as simple as that, of course, when the biographer never knew the person he is attempting to describe and has to recover him by means of research and historical imagination. He can never be quite sure that he has found him. But what the historically-minded biographer tries to do is to live with his subject in spirit long enough and intimately enough to form definite impressions of the proportions of his character and personality. Then, when he runs across some incident, savory or unsavory, he can judge whether or not it is in character—whether it is a proper illustration of the nature of the man or is largely without significance. His use of such an incident would depend, not primarily on its appeal to the interest of the reader, but on his mature judgment as to its appropriateness.

In the course of my own studies I have come across some lurid stories about the personal life of Thomas Jefferson. These would make a chapter which would be read with avidity. One of my tasks is to try to determine whether or not these stories are true. Most of them emanated from a single poisoned source, the vitriolic pen of an unscrupulous journalist who had turned upon his benefactor; and most of them are not true. But let us say that some of them are true—Jefferson himself admitted that one was. Nonetheless, it is my strong impression that he was fastidiously clean in his personal life. He was extraordinarily devoted to his wife while she was living and reverent of her memory after her early death, and he lavished upon his motherless daughters a tenderness which is hard to describe without sentimentality. What, then, shall I do with an unsavory incident which, in my opinion, is out of character? The only thing I am sure of is that I should not accentuate it. Much depends on the length of the biography I am writing, but at all events I must try to depict the man in the proportions which I have perceived. These proportions may not be correct, for my judgment is fallible; they may not seem precisely the same to any two students; but it is my obligation to see them as clearly and as honestly as I can.

On the *Dictionary of American Biography* one of our constant problems was what to do with the "dirt." It would have been a great convenience to have a rule of thumb but we never found one. Each case had to be judged on its own merits. We claimed no supreme wisdom but sometimes we deliberately put some "dirt" in, and sometimes we deliberately took some out. Insofar as we had any rule at all, it was that derelictions in matters of public concern were more important than private immorality. This is in direct contrast to the general popular tendency to forgive a man for crookedness in office because he is a devoted husband and a kind father. Whether or not a man got drunk upon occasion may not have been significant, though it may have been; while abuse of public trust may generally be assumed to be important. The personal morals of a clergyman are unquestionably more important to his career than are those of a soldier, and stories about statesmen that are whispered around have historical significance whenever they affect the public mind. As a rule, however, the public morality of a man is more important than the private. Furthermore, we were always confronted with the problem of proportion. Occasional scandalous references do not mar the proportions of a long article, while one such reference might throw a short one badly out of balance.

The so-called "debunking" of the post-war decade cannot be blamed primarily upon the influence of the novelists, for the spirit from which it grew was present in sober historians. At its best it represented a fearless effort to expose error; and no one can deny that the sweeping away of old prejudices and superstitions served to blow the fog from many a mind. It is rather shocking, however, now that we can look back, to realize how negative so many of us were and what negativeness we fostered. As William James has pointed out, many scholars spend more effort in avoiding error than in seeking truth. Some of us who as historians were so eager to banish error thought ourselves boldly aggressive, little realizing that we were helping create a vacuum and plunging into it.

The measured judgment of the historian should include praise for the praiseworthy as well as blame for those who deserve it. There can be no scholarly objection to the exposure of the foibles and peccadillos of the Fathers of the Republic, and there is strong reason for the exposure of the inadequacy of statesmanship or of any sort of leadership whenever it is observed, but we owe it to our countrymen, as well as to the Fathers, to measure their services as a whole. Nothing that has yet been revealed about Samuel Adams or Patrick Henry or the rest of the Patriots has caused me personally to doubt that as a group they deserved well of their country; nothing that has yet been brought forward as a necessary corrective of an unfair attitude toward the Loyalists has convinced me that they are to be preferred. I could doubtless quicken your interest by telling some trivial story about George Washington to show that, after all, he had foibles like other men, and I am sure that he is big enough to stand it. But no biographer of Washington has any right to obscure the major fact that his greatness was that of character. Said Mr. Justice Holmes to Sir Frederick Pollock: "Belittling arguments always have a force of their own, but you and I believe that high-mindedness is not impossible to man." (June 30, 1928.) [3] Without surrendering our critical faculties we can accept the observation of Carlyle as profoundly true: "No sadder proof can be

[3] Mark D. Howe, Ed., *Holmes-Pollock Letters* (Cambridge, Mass., 1941), II, 223 (June 30, 1928).

given by any man of his own littleness than disbelief in great men."

The sad truth is that everybody likes a bit of scandal and that we all gain a sort of sadistic delight in contemplating the frailties of others. Once having conceived of biography as designed to entertain the public, any writer is subjected to strong temptations to appeal to the weaknesses of human nature. If he has no fear of the sober judgment of the guild of scholars and is a man of untrained judgment or facile conscience, he may easily become reckless.

It is not surprising, therefore, that the popularization of biography involved to a considerable extent its commercialization and resulted in the display of a vast amount of trash, along with some jewels of literary art. The emphasis on form rather than facts was dangerous in the hands of irresponsible persons, and the general impression was created that any facile writer could create an acceptable biography without excessive labor. It is unfortunate that some term like "fictional biography" did not come into general use as the term "historical fiction" has. The line of demarcation between historical biography and fictional biography may not always be clear, and certainly not to the ordinary reader, but unquestionably such a line exists. The person who should be most conscious of it is the writer himself. It may be too much to expect that in every biographical work there be a foreword, displaying the same sort of candor that is normally expected of historical scholars by stating just what the author claims and does not claim to do. It is hard to see how a pure-publishing act could be drawn or enforced, but every article that is displayed to the public ought to bear an honest label.

The effects of the emphasis on interest, however, were not wholly evil. Humanizing influences were released and these had perceptible influence on the work and writing of scholars. In the course of time there was a reaction against the extreme fictional forms and there has been in our day a marked revival of what may truly be termed historical biography. What part the *Dictionary of American Biography* may have played in this, it is not for me to say. It seems reasonable to suppose, however, that some of the 2,000 contributors to that cooperative work must have been encouraged to make other ventures in the biographical field and must have been influenced to some extent by the standards of humanized scholarship which so many of us attempted to maintain. Biographical titles appeared in increasing number on lists of doctoral dissertations. The main reason for this may have been the growing scarcity of subjects, but a change in the attitude of the professionals was also reflected. Meanwhile, certain amateurs, without benefit of graduate instruction, attained a status which deserves to be described as professional.

Said André Maurois in 1929: "A bad Victorian biography is a formless mass of ill-digested matter; a bad modern biography is a book of spurious fame animated by a would-be ironic spirit which is merely cruel and shallow."[4] In recent years there has been a strong though not universal tendency to avoid the two extremes. Much scholarly writing in all the humanistic

[4] *Aspects of Biography* (Cambridge, England, 1929), p. 8.

fields has continued to be formless and to abound in quotations which are even easier for a reader to skip than they are for an author to transcribe. But an increasing number of scholars of high integrity are aware that if they are going to tell a story there is every reason why they should try to tell it well. They also realize better than they used to that actors on the stage of history are not colorless figures of cardboard but human beings. Accordingly, they are more disposed to weave important details of personal information into the text, instead of ignoring them entirely or relegating them to the obscurity of a footnote. Both in form and content the historical biography of our day reflects the influence of the school of fiction.

Perhaps I am too sanguine, but it seems to me that our biographical writing as a whole is on a sounder and more realistic basis than in times past. And if relatively few biographies now sell like novels, the degree of popular success and public recognition which has been accorded some of the works of sound scholarship is distinctly encouraging. The public may still like jazz and swing but there is also a growing appreciation of good music. To cite but a single example, we may well take courage when a book like Douglas Freeman's *R. E. Lee* is not only awarded a Pulitzer prize but also appears on the best-seller lists.

There is really no such thing as biography, of course; there are only biographies. These may and should be as diverse as the human lives they portray; but there is a large common denominator, for in many respects the pattern of human existence everywhere and at all times is essentially the same. Biographers may come from any field of learning or from no technical field at all, but they face similar problems, wherever they come from. Accordingly, it is possible to point out some of the prime requisites of biography, and to suggest its chief limitations and its major potentialities.

To begin with, a biography should orientate its subject in history, though it should certainly not contain a full story of the times. The man himself must be kept in the center of the stage. A biographer can easily say too much about the setting and the other actors, but he can hardly know too much about them. It is for this reason that amateurs are suspect in what we have termed historical biography, and that they cannot perform their tasks without becoming in effect professionals, whatever their nominal label may be. The situation is distinctly different in contemporary biography, for a great many other people may understand their own age just as well as the historians do, or even better.

In the second place, what a man did must be told. Some have asserted that they want to know not so much what a man did as why he did it. In the case of familiar figures, like William Shakespeare or Abraham Lincoln, it may be that there is less need for new information than for fresh interpretation. However, an interpretive essay is not biography in the full sense, and if any author has spared himself all the trouble of grubbing with his own hands for facts he ought to say so. There is every reason for a biographer to answer the questions, "why" and "how," if he can; but these questions never would be asked if a person had not done something. The importance of deeds does vary with individuals. The physical movements of William James are less important than his mental processes, while the reverse is true of John Paul Jones. As a rule the narrative element should predominate, and any biography has intrinsic justification if it truthfully tells a good story.

However, there must be value-judgments and these constitute requirement number three. The extent to which these should be explicitly expressed depends upon the subject and the nature of his career, and also upon the character of the audience. This is a question which has to be decided in each individual case on artistic and pedagogical grounds. A well-told tale may point its own moral; and the artist who has patiently painted in the lights and shadows may never be able to tell, in so many words, all that a portrait reveals. But, no matter how industrious he may have been in investigation, the biographer cannot escape the obligation of thought and judgment. In his own mind he must take and keep on taking the measure of his man. Biography that abounds in hasty judgment on insufficient evidence is false, but biography that is devoid of judgment is vain.

Finally, so far as personal elements and factors are concerned, the more authentic information that can be obtained the more adequate the interpretation is likely to be. Parentage and grandparentage are of the first importance, though remote ancestry in the paternal line is important chiefly in the history of the name. From the scientific point of view, it is obviously absurd to single out one line to the exclusion of the others. It is a pity that no more authentic information is available about the mothers of great men and the crucial early years of nurture. In this respect recent figures are better subjects of full biography.

Marriage and children are generally important, but in varying degree. For a soldier or sailor, whose great deeds are performed away from home, family details may amount to little; while the career of a literary man, who works at home amid the howling of his progeny, may be profoundly affected by domestic circumstances. Much literary hackwork may be explained in the simple, human terms of the size and needs of the writer's family. Indeed, one need not be an economic determinist to recognize that important clues to human conduct and character may be revealed by an examination of the stubs of check-books. For the old days, unfortunately, they do not exist and one must seek the best available substitute.

Personal appearance is generally of interest but, while it is significant in the careers of Daniel Webster, William Jennings Bryan, and Edwin Booth, it is relatively unimportant in the career of a mathematician and physicist like Willard Gibbs or of almost any scientist. Physical condition, on the other hand, is almost always important. The physical collapse of Woodrow Wilson had an appreciable effect on the destiny of nations. Medical diaries would be invaluable but unhappily they do not exist even for men now living. As to sex life, I will agree with a magazine writer of several years ago that it is important only if pathological; otherwise, like a good digestion, it may be assumed. It was significant in the career of Lafcadio Hearn but hardly in that of Robert E. Lee. And in practically no cases are the full facts available.

Thus do the scientific limitations of biography appear. In his efforts to procure factual materials the investigator must be as laborious and painstaking as any historian and he must be equally honest in interpreting them. In this sense it may be said that he should have the scientific spirit. But it is hard to conceive of any circumstances in which the facts that he discovers will be complete or that his interpretation of them will be accorded scientific standing. Indeed, the statistics which can be drawn from such a comprehensive work as the *Dictionary of American Biography*, however suggestive these may be to students of heredity and environment and of ethnic groups, are too fragmentary to serve as a basis for scientific generalization.

Biography can hardly be regarded as a science, either social, natural, or biological. I prefer to think of it as an art but here also there are definite limitations, for its materials, distressingly fragmentary though they so often are, lack the flexibility and malleability of the materials of fiction. Facts may not always be absolute or indubitable, but stubborn they unquestionably are, and the biographical artist must work within the confines of what he believes to be the truth. The proportions which he discovers may not be graceful but ungainly. In biography, truth is not necessarily beauty, nor is beauty truth; often they are clearly distinguishable. Being a portrait painter has its disadvantages. As

Virginia Woolf has said, if truth be thought of as having "granite-like solidity," and personality as having "rainbow-like intangibility," the problem of welding the two is so difficult that it often seems insoluble.

Nonetheless, the biographer labors in a field of almost limitless potentiality. His materials are as diverse as human life and just as fascinating. In the recorded history of the United States alone can be found heroes and villains of every hue. Here is the effective answer to the scandal-monger and the satirist. There is no need to distort the truth even if one wishes to be dramatic, for fact can be discovered that is far stranger than fiction. Let me illustrate by calling a small part of our American roll and thus revealing its challenging diversity. Here are subjects for any taste.

There have been pioneers in the trackless wilderness like Daniel Boone and George Rogers Clark: there have been pioneers in the pathless air like Wilbur and Orville Wright. The adventurous outlaw Jean Lafitte, born in France, preyed on the commerce of the Gulf: he was hardly more predatory than the adventurous promoter Charles W. Morse, born in the State of Maine and afterwards called "The Admiral of the Atlantic Coast," who was committed to the Atlanta penitentiary, and, owing to various incredible circumstances, was freed for further depredations. We have had railroad builders like James J. Hill, and railroad wreckers like Jay Gould, Jim Fisk, and Daniel Drew. The famous Texas cattleman, Charles Goodnight, acquired some million acres of land and 100,000 cattle; a great executive of the Standard Oil Company, Henry Clay Folger, amassed a fortune and proceeded to acquire more than 70,000 volumes and other items dealing with Shakespeare, and made available to literary scholars the finest Shakespearean collection in the world.

America gave birth to the renowned classicist Basil L Gildersleeve, a serene Olympian: she gave scope to the sensational journalistic career of the Hungarian, Joseph Pulitzer, whose eager impetuosity is revealed by the story that he jumped from his incoming boat and swam to the dock in Boston. Thomas Nast, the cartoonist, born in Germany, invented the Republican elephant and the Democratic donkey, twisted the tail of the Tammany tiger, and made James G. Blaine forever ridiculous by depicting him with a tall plume in his top hat: Saint-Gaudens, the sculptor, born of French and Irish parents in Dublin, designed an unforgettable monument to the wife of his friend Henry Adams and immortalized Abraham Lincoln in stone. The Yankee, Eli Whitney, came south and invented a gin, which in less than a decade caused the production of cotton to increase more than two hundredfold: the Virginian, Cyrus Hall McCormick, invented a reaper in his native valley, went to Chicago, to manufacture and sell it, and unintentionally, through this revolutionary machine, facilitated the victory of the north in the Civil War.

President Charles W. Eliot was a New Englander of the New Englanders, and presumably, of pure English stock: President Henry Suzzalo of the University of Washington and the Carnegie Foundation stated that in his veins was not one drop of Anglo-Saxon blood.

Abraham Lincoln claimed that you cannot fool all the people all the time: P. T. Barnum and his circus demonstrated that upon occasion a large portion of it likes to be taken in. From Vermont came Lincoln's rival, Stephen A. Douglas, Calvin Coolidge, and the founder of Mormonism, Joseph Smith. William Dean Howells, editor of the *Atlantic* and the *Century* and first president of the American Academy of Arts and Letters, never went beyond the grammar school: both Woodrow Wilson and Henry Cabot Lodge were Ph.D's. Benjamin Franklin, one of seventeen children and the youngest son of the youngest son for five generations, arrived in Philadelphia with a Dutch dollar and a shilling in copper: Franklin Roosevelt, born to wealth, was an only child. Andrew Johnson was a tailor, Cornelius Vanderbilt ran a ferryboat, and Andrew Carnegie began as a bobbin boy. Carry Nation who was nearly six feet tall and weighed 175 pounds, sought to advance the cause of temperance by wrecking saloons: Dr. Mary E. Walker sought to aid in the emancipation of women by wearing trousers, little realizing that the time would come when feminine apparel could be discarded with impunity.

In dealing with persons such as these, there is opportunity to employ not merely such talents as are adapted to the *American Historical Review*, but also such as are displayed in the *New Yorker*.

Biography is personalized history and by means of it the heritage of the past can be immeasurably enriched. In itself it may reveal no universal law but unquestionably it can help us understand the varieties of human behavior; and, since it deals with the conspicuous rather than with the commonplace, it should provide clues to the unsolved mystery of leadership. On other grounds, however, its appeal may be expected to be perennial: nothing that is human is foreign to its province.

THEOLOGY OF HISTORY

By *GEORGE LA PIANA*

Theology of History

THE Christian religion, breaking away from Judaism, made its appearance in the Greco-Roman world as a mystery of salvation and advanced the claim of being a universal religion. Against the ancient tradition which considered religion as an essential part of the *mores patrii*, and a strictly national property, Christianity professed a universalism which knew no national boundaries and no class distinctions. It has been remarked that this universalism of Christianity implied a vision of history based on spiritual and moral values which were not the exclusive property of this or that people or nation but were common to all mankind; and, as a consequence, that against the particularism and nationalism of the ancient and classical historical tradition, Christianity introduced the notion of universal history. *"Ubique patria, ubique lex et religio mea est,"* said Paulus Orosius, who in the fifth century was the first to write a history on a tentative universal plan.

It is well known that Orosius wrote his history at the suggestion of St. Augustine, who in the *City of God* had set down an ideal plan and a method for the interpretation of history. The *City of God* has been called and is still called by many the first and greatest book of philosophy of history ever produced by Christian civilization. The historical pattern elaborated by Augustine became the model for Christian historiography of medieval and modern times, and from it a large section of contemporary Christian historical works still take their inspiration. It seems, however, that the term "philosophy of history" as applied to this and similar methods of historical interpretation is altogether misleading. More properly, this type of philosophy of history is a theology of history, inasmuch as its fundamental premises, on which the whole structure is built and stands, come from religious beliefs and from their theological elaborations about the nature of the universe, of man and his destiny. History written from this point of view becomes apologetics.

The method of history suggested or imposed by theological premises cannot be other than a theological method. It remains fundamentally a theological method even when the historians who follow it use the most refined instruments supplied by modern historical criticism in dealing with specific problems or aspects of history.

The theological method of history reigned supreme for many centuries and is still that of many general and special histories written today, but it found its highest application and its most complete development in religious history. This was only natural, since this was the field in which the connection between theological beliefs and the facts of history was expected to be the closest, and in which the facts were expected to be the demonstration of the theories.

The plan of this paper is to analyze first the fundamental premises of theology of history, then to see how they affected the method and purposes of history-writing, and finally to consider the attitude of the modern mind toward theology of history in the light of contemporary events.

The four pillars which support the whole structure of theology of history are four great myths or concrete representations of abstract notions and beliefs and of social and religious experiences.

1. The myth of a divine revelation as an external historical fact, which took place in time and space and through which men were taught truths that they never could have discovered by themselves.

2. The myth of the golden age and the fall of man, by which human life and human society, which had been created perfect and free from all evil, were now considered as degraded to a condition in which evil was an essential constitutive part of their nature, to be removed only through redemption by a divine agent.

3. The myth of the divine origin of authority in all its forms, political as well as religious.

4. The myth of the chosen people, by which a people, either in the ethnical sense or as members of a religious institutional body were considered the object of special and exclusive predilection by the superhuman powers and charged by them with a special and exclusive mission in the world.

It is not my intention to discuss the problem of the origin of these myths or to trace their growth within primitive societies; this problem has its proper place in dealing with the origin of religion. Neither am I concerned with the theoretical and apologetical question as to whether their claim to have an objective validity —their claim to be objective realities—may or may not be justified on religious and theological grounds. For our purposes such a discussion is wholly unnecessary. To the historian these myths are but human interpretations of facts and experiences of life. They are historical facts only as far as they had and still have a subjective existence in the minds and the consciousness of men, only as far as they appear as traditional constitutive elements of human thinking handed down from generation to generation, only as far as they supplied and still supply motives and purposes to the actions and deeds of peoples and nations in the making of their history.

As all the creations of human thought, the notion, the form, and the content of these myths have undergone a long process of development during which they assumed different connotations and different meanings, according to times and places and according to the intellectual and social level reached in human history. Starting from crude, primitive, magical notions, they assumed in time the form of concrete realities in the mythological world and they found their highest expression in poetry and religious rituals. Still later they reached the stage in which they were subjected to a more thorough intellectual re-elaboration, and here poetry became philosophy and mythology became theology. Meanwhile, through all these ascending steps of their evolution, they sank deeper and deeper into human individual and social consciousness; they became traditions firmly rooted in the mental habits of men and found expression in religious and political institutions, in literature and art, in philosophy and sciences; and, last but not least, they came to be looked upon as universal historical premises from which all attempts to write the history of human events necessarily had to start. They became the guiding light in discriminating between truth and error, between good and evil, and provided human history with a soul, with a meaning and a purpose.

It is important also to remark that the more this intellectual re-elaboration of the myths advanced, the more the myth of revelation came to hold a central position. As the most universal principle providing a common basis for all the others, it became the pivot around which revolved human history in all its phases and in all its aspects. The myth of revelation, which may have started with such simple forms as dreams and visions connected with the notion of powers different from and above the human powers, in time came to be conceived in terms of communications and relations with a superhuman world of gods who spoke to men through divination and oracles, and then through commandments and rules of action given directly, as were those given to Moses on Mount Sinai.

The mythological elaboration established still closer connections through the stories of divine beings assuming human form, living among men and sharing human passions and pleasures, and finally of gods who went themselves through the tragic experience of death and resurrection, opening thus to mortal men the door to blessed immortality.

Last but not least, old writings, rituals and poetry, sacred legends and chronicles, imaginary biographies and bits of folklore gathered in books, came to be considered as having a supernatural origin and containing in a fixed and definite form that revelation which was formerly in a fluid state and subject to the vicissitudes of oral tradition. Each of the various systems of revelation represented by sets of sacred books claimed to be the only true revelation and the final revelation, after which there should be no other. Each one of them claimed to be complete and exhaustive, covering with its theoretical teaching and its normative commandments all aspects of life, all human activities of the individual as well as of organized groups. Being the product of divine wisdom, these sacred books were not only the teachers of theological beliefs and ritual practices, but also the repositories of all knowledge; they were codes of ethics; they were the only authoritative source from which principles of law and government, social and economic rules affecting all conditions and classes, could and should be derived.

The Christian religion inherited all these notions of revelation from its predecessors, made them its own, perfected and harmonized them in its own theological system. But Christianity went much farther than all other religions in extending the notion of revelation to cover not only its doctrines and its religious ritual, its laws and its ethics, but also the institutional expression of these ideas in the Church, with its hierarchy, its constitution and its traditions. In other words, revelation in Christianity came to be embodied primarily in the

Church, which claimed thus a divine origin for its organization and its authority and the actual immanent assistance of the Holy Spirit as an invisible divine power which inspired and guided the visible Church and prevented it from falling into error and evil.

The myth of the golden age and the following degradation of mankind was the mythological answer to the baffling question why men are subject to suffering and death and to evil in all its forms. It seemed unreasonable and impossible that such was the original destiny of mankind. The imagination pictured a happy age of perfection and joy in the faraway past, and then the tragic story of guilt incurred, punished, and still to be expiated. This myth could even be clothed with the purple mantle of philosophy, as in the metaphysical speculations of Plato, but it remained essentially the human reaction against the limitations of the physical and intellectual nature of man.

The experience of the inevitability of evil and of its unaccountable nature suggested also the explanation that the dualism of good and evil in the world was merely the reflection of a dualism in the eternal source of life itself. As in the Iranian religious tradition, this dualism was expressed in concrete mythological figures and assumed the form of a cosmic epic struggle between the gods of light and the gods of darkness, a struggle of which mankind was the prize. In this dualistic vision of universal life, the golden age, which in the myth of the fall of man had been located back in the remote past, was shifted to a remote future. The golden age was to come when the powers of darkness should be defeated and destroyed by the powers of light and all evil should disappear forever.

Christianity here again inherited these myths, made them its own, and combined them in its theological and moral system. The myth of the fall of man inherited from Judaism, which in the religion of Israel played a very small and unimportant part, in Christianity assumed the position of keystone of the whole dogmatic structure. It provided the basis for its counterpart, the myth of redemption. But the myth of redemption in its turn presupposed a dualistic background and a conflict of enemy powers. According to the doctrine of redemption which for so long dominated Christian theology, men were all slaves of Satan as a consequence of Adam's sin. To free men from their abject slavery, a tragic conflict must take place, in which the son of God himself had to die on the cross, and then rise from the dead and thus triumph over Satan.

Through this amalgamation of the myth of the fall of man and the dualistic myth of redemption, Christianity accepted also both views of the golden age: there had been a golden age at the beginning before Adam's sin and there would be a golden age in the future when Christ should return on earth to establish his kingdom. But, strange as it may seem, Christianity in spite of its rigid theoretical monotheism and in spite of the universal implication of its myth of redemption, did not reach the logical conclusion of universal salvation and of the final and total destruction of evil, as we find in Zoroastrianism, but with its doctrine of the eternity of hell assigned an everlasting existence to evil and suffering.

The ancient dualistic myth assigned to evil an eternal origin, but refused to it an eternal existence in the future; Christianity reversed the situation: it denied to evil an eternal source but it granted to it a permanent immortality.

But there was another and no less important result of this syncretism of myths in the Christian system. In the hands of the theologians, and especially of St. Augustine, the myth of the fall of man developed into the doctrine of original sin and the total organic depravity of human nature. In this tragic myth of human degradation and inherited guilt and of redemption limited by predestination, we find merged and flowing together the most diverse and conflicting elements: mythological traditions and beliefs, cosmological theories and mysteriosophic theophanies, monotheism and dualism, leading to an anthropology in which freedom of will and responsibility rub elbows with determinism and predestination; total depravity with the positive obligation of doing good; divine grace, which by definition is irresistible, with the human capacity of resisting and spurning grace; liberty of choice with fatalism— all combined in the most amazing syncretism ever conceived by mortal minds. And last but not least, the great divine drama of redemption in which God himself plays the leading role by assuming human flesh and dying on the cross, in spite of its cosmic universal value ends with the salvation of only a few selected souls, while the multitude remain in the clutches of a tormented but still triumphant Satan.

A very old myth of the theology of history is that which in its earlier form may be described as the divine origin of kings. According to mythological genealogies, which were different in details but substantially identical, a divine blood ran through the veins of kings and hence all powers were theirs by a congenital right, not only the power to rule and exact obedience but even such divine powers as those of healing diseases and working miracles.

When this physical connection of dynasties with superhuman beings began to seem too naive and too awkward to be taken literally, the myth underwent a process of re-elaboration and assumed the form which could be properly called an *adoptionist dynastic theology*. Though the ruler had ceased to be a god, he partook still of the divine prerogatives. He was still in close communion with the universal powers and was admitted to share the honors due to them. A significant example of this kind of dynastic adoptionism is the Roman notion of the Genius of the Emperor, a divine embodiment of the eternity of the Roman power and of the Roman wisdom. The emperor, irrespective of his personal qualities, was the adopted visible form of the Genius of the Imperium and at his death was enumerated among the gods by an official apotheosis.

It is important to notice that throughout all this development there was no distinction between a supreme religious and a supreme political authority; the two were identified and resided in the same person as inseparable powers derived at the same time from the same source. It was with Christianity that the dichotomy of spiritual and temporal as two separate political and social realms made its entrance in history. In this new dualism the highest place was claimed by the priestly authority as having a more direct divine origin, as the guardian and dispenser of spiritual values, and as the only agency of salvation, which is the supreme end of life. To the temporal authority and its representatives was assigned a lower place, since their task was limited and subsidiary to that of the Church.

But even so, the old myth of the divine origin of rulers did not cease to exist altogether. Starting from the general principle that all authority comes from God, even in Christianity the political ruler could still claim to be the depositary and the instrument of the will of God and the executor of God's plans. Recognized as such, he too assumed a semi-religious character, he too received the charismatic unction which lifted him into the circle of sacred beings. And finally, when most of the old external forms of royal canonization were thrown overboard with the post medieval secularization of culture and politics, the old myth refused to die and remained stubbornly on its pedestal, disguised under the juridical doctrine of the divine right of kings.

It is needless to say that in the Church the old myth had a more complete fulfillment, to the point of vesting human personalities with the overpowering functions of dispensing divine grace and even of acting as the vicars of God on earth.

The last of the great myths of theology of history is the myth of the chosen people. The classical example of this myth is that of the people of Israel, but it is very important to remark that the myth was by no means peculiar only to that people either in ancient or in modern times. In societies which had reached a monotheistic conception of God, this myth was a survival of an earlier stage, when the god was a limited local tribal god who owned that people as his only exclusive divine domain on earth, and who in his turn was owned as the special and exclusive property of that people. When, as it happened in Israel, by the rise of moral ideas having implicitly a universal value, the originally tribal god assumed the place of a universal and unique god, the old notion of that bilateral ownership was carried over and was adapted to the new context. Notice that of the two parts of the old notion of mutual ownership, of the people by the god and of the god by the people, the second, which was carried over in the form that the chosen people has a special claim over the universal god, was and remained the stronger as a psychological motive which determined the history and the destiny of that people.

Less conspicuous but no less real was the active function that this myth performed in the history of other peoples, such as the Greeks and the Romans. The special and unique mission assigned by the gods to the Greeks was to create and to teach to the world culture, sense of beauty, harmony of plastic forms, literature, philosophy, art. They were the people chosen to save the world by knowledge. They had inherited the divine fire stolen by Prometheus from Olympus, they were the salt of the earth, the Hellenes: all other peoples and races were merely barbarians. Proclus, the last of the pagan philosophers, could with reason address to Minerva-Athena his famous prayer: "It is thou who hast opened to us the divine doors of wisdom and tamed the race of giants. Thy throne is on the Acropolis. . . . Thou cherisheth this our land of redemption, this mother of books . . . this center of irradiation of thy divine light. Thou hast entrusted to it thy thoughts and thy divine wisdom."

Among the Romans we find again the same claim of being the only chosen people, but on different grounds. Every Roman boy was taught by his pedagogue to say with the poet: "Remember, O Roman, that thou art born to rule the world." The mission of Rome, willed and abetted by the gods, was to conquer and to rule the world; conquer it by the strength of its armies and rule it by the wisdom of its law. Rome with its law, the highest creation of the Roman genius, was to secure order, peace, and prosperity to the world for ever. *"Alme sol, possis nihil urbe Roma visere majus."*

Need we go over the whole of history to find evidence that this myth, from the medieval *Gesta Dei per Francos* to the modern *Deutschland über alles,* has never ceased to haunt the imagination and to inflame the passions, the greed, and the pride of peoples and nations?

With Christianity, however, this myth assumed a new form, by shifting altogether the principle and its implications from a national and racial to a strictly religious ground. As I have already mentioned, in ancient history each religion, its beliefs, its ritual and its institutions, were an essential part of the *mores patrii*, and its gods were the gods of the land. The notion of a religion with no national connection was extraneous to the ancient world. The universal tolerance of the Roman government toward all religions and cults was not dictated by philosophical considerations, but by the juridical tradition which respected the *patrii mores*. But Christianity, breaking away from Judaism, recruited its followers among peoples of all races and nations, and hence it became a religion with no national connections.

The consciousness of this disability led the Christians from the very beginning to advance the claim that they too were a people, a new people. This idea was very forcibly expressed in the first Epistle of Peter: "We are a chosen race, a royal priesthood, a holy nation, and a special people." Tertullian even made a serious attempt to convince the Roman magistrates that the Christians were a nation. In his *Apologeticum* he propounded the theory that the privileges and exemptions the Roman government granted to the Jews must be taken away from them and granted to the Christians, because all the prophecies and the expectations which constituted the essence of the Jewish religion had been realized in Christianity, so that Christianity was thus the true Israel and the inheritor of all the rights of Israel. Christianity, says Tertullian, is a "*tertium genus*," a third race, formed by the merging of the two other races, the Jewish and the Gentile, to constitute the new chosen people, the true people of God.

All these four great myths are fundamentally related expressions of the same theological notion that the universe, visible and invisible, that man and his world, are more or less passive tools in the hands of super-human powers and that these powers are embodied in or represented by selected human beings who are at the same time passive and active instruments of a divine will. There is another general notion which these myths have also in common, a notion that is of fundamental importance in the theology of history, and this is the assumption that the earth, this little speck of dust, and man, this little animal that crawls over it, are the central object of God's care in the universe. It was for man that God created everything. For the salvation of man this God, whose being, power, and splendor no human mind can comprehend, much less describe, sent his son, God consubstantial, to become a man and to die on the cross. The little speck of dust was thus transfigured by a divine light more brilliant than the light of all the constellations of heaven, and man, the little animal, raised himself to the level of God.

Throughout all the centuries of our Christian civilization, history was conceived and written on the presupposition that these myths represented eternal truths and embodied God's plans and purposes in the universe. The narrative of historical events, their meaning and value, all moral and political judgments passed upon rulers, governments, upon policies and achievements or failures, were all determined a priori by the relation, either of agreement or of divergence, in which they stood to the principle and the implications of revelation, of man's sinful nature and of Christian redemption, of the divine origin of authority and the divine exclusive mission of the Church.

But it was in religious and ecclesiastical history that the theological method had its widest and most thorough application. The first model of this method of history goes back to the ancient Church and to the first attempt to describe the birth and early growth of Christianity in the early centuries, the *Ecclesiastical History* of Eusebius of Caesarea. In the first chapter of his history Eusebius developed the theory that Christianity is the oldest religion of the world, because Christ existed from eternity and equally from eternity existed the Church in God's mind. The Church is the central point in which the whole history of the universe converges: all the events which preceded its foundation were in preparation of the establishment of the Church, "*preparatio evangelica*"; all the events which accompanied and followed the establishment of the Church are the realization of all past hopes, "*demonstratio evangelica*," and at the same time the preparation of the final scene of the great cosmic drama, the final judgment and the reabsorption of the Church into the celestrial Jerusalem, "*consummatio saeculi*." Having set this background, Eusebius fitted into it his narrative.

Here Eusebius's guiding light was orthodoxy, that is to say, the body of doctrines and beliefs which had begun to crystallize in official formulae at that time, the beginning of the fourth century. Those beliefs and doctrines were the result of a long process of elaboration in which, among endless conflicts and controversies, Christian thought had reinterpreted its original beliefs by the process of assimilation and exclusion under the influence of various factors. But to Eusebius the orthodox doctrine, instead of being the point of arrival of the whole historical development, was its point of departure; orthodoxy was a divine revelation which existed in the same form and with the same meaning from the very beginning; it was the teaching of Jesus and of his apostles.

Eusebius's historical task thus became very simple. The long conflicts, doubts, and hesitations of Christian thought during the early centuries, which were the result of the painful effort to give intelligible and rational form to beliefs which smacked so much of mythology, such as that Jesus was God and man at the same time, in Eusebius's narrative became conscious and willful attempts to deviate from the revealed truth. Eusebius did not and could not realize that heresy was older than orthodoxy. Behind every heretic he could always spot the grinning face of Mephistopheles, happy to play havoc in the church of God.

This is the pattern of the theological method of history which, with minor changes and adaptations, remained the only approved orthodox approach to religious and ecclesiastical history. Many centuries after Eusebius, the eloquent and learned French bishop Bossuet in his *Discourse on Universal History*, as well as in his *Variations of the Protestant Church,* summarized his historical method in this aphorism which he addressed to the Protestants: "Do you introduce changes and innovations? Then you are in error." ("*Mutas? ergo erras.*") The myth of revelation does not allow any other method of history but the method which starts from the principle of the perpetuity and the immutability of dogma from which nothing essential can be subtracted and to which nothing essential can be added. To be sure, Christianity, like all other religions which claimed to possess the final revelation, could not prevent within its own system further evolutions and changes according to changing intellectual and social conditions. But these changes, instead of assuming the character of new revelations, were grafted into the old system by the way of interpretation. The art of pouring new wine into old bottles has never reached such perfection as with the interpreters and the historians of divine revelation.

The bearing of the myth of the fall of man and of redemption on the theological method of history was no less important. The pessimistic notion of human nature and the capital role assigned to divine grace and predestination implied not only a static conception of history, but also a view of life filled with fear and a sense of helplessness. The dichotomy of salvation and damnation depending not upon human choice or human effort, but upon divine grace and predestination, divided mankind into two sections, which Augustine called the *City of God* and the *City of Satan.* These coexist in time and space, but they form two different and opposite realms. To the City of God belong all men who set the love of God above all things and who practice self-denial and altruism; to the City of Satan belong all others, who put in first place the love of self and who seek after pleasure with the utmost selfishness. "Tell me what is that you love, and I will tell you of what city you are a citizen." A lofty conception derived from the purest moral sources of Christian spirituality!

As historical realities, the two cities would be like two rivers flowing in parallel lines, but never mixing their waters, coming from different sources and ending one in the ocean of divinity and the other in the marshes of Acheron. The line which divides one city from the other cuts across all institutional and social boundaries of life, so that to belong to the Church or even to hold high ecclesiastical office does not imply belonging to the City of God. In other words, God alone knows those boundaries, because only he knows those whom he has selected and those whom he has rejected.

When in the year A.D. 410 Rome—which from the time of Brenner had never again seen hostile armies attack its walls—was taken by the Goths, the pagans raised the outcry that this catastrophe had happened because Rome had forsaken its own gods to worship the god of a foreign superstition, Christianity. Why, they asked, why did Rome when a pagan city prosper and conquer, and now that it had become a Christian city was it violated and abandoned to the sword of the barbarians? The gods did nothing for Rome because the gods do not exist, replied Augustine. It was the only true God who bestowed prosperity and power on the Romans and who now is letting them suffer according to his plans.

But why, insisted the pagans, why, when Rome was conquered and sacked by the barbarians were Christian men and women massacred and Christian virgins dragged out of their monasteries, raped, and killed by the savage soldiers? Where was their God? Why did he not save his own people? God was there when those things happened, replied Augustine. He was there and he let some of them be killed as a punishment for their sins, and he left his virgins to be raped to try and purify their souls by the fire of suffering and death.

This is a highly distilled theology of history leading to the conclusion that every human event is a mystery and that every attempt to interpret or explain human events is a strictly theological task to be undertaken by those who are confident that they can read between the lines of God's plans and purposes for the world.

Neither does Augustine escape from the strictures of historical determinism. His academic distinction between *libertas* and *liberum arbitrium* does not destroy the fact that human agents under the law of predestination have no choice in their actions. No theological subtlety and no psychological sophistry can overcome the contradiction. To apply to men the burden of moral responsibility, because God has given them the knowledge that they are agents of evil, while the same God has denied them the power to react against evil, is, if anything, a fatal blow to Augustine's fundamental notion of God as a moral will and to his distinction between the City of God and the City of Satan. The Augustinian methodology of history is pure theology; history, like theology, is a divine mystery and it shall be understood and written only by heavenly historians.

Augustine did not identify the City of God with the Church, though in many passages of the last section of his book he applied to the Church some of the qualifications of the City of God. But this identification, which could not fit well into Augustine's spiritual and mystical conception of the City of God, was possible and feasible under the myth of the divine origin of the Church. A religious institution claiming a direct and immediate divine origin, claiming the permanent assistance of the Holy Spirit, and hence distinguished by the characteristics of holiness, of universality and uniqueness, of indefectibility and infallibility, could very well be called the City of God.

This City of God, the Church, as the mystical body of Christ and the repository of divine grace, had a spiritual existence of its own over and above the visible congregation of the faithful. The Church thus anticipated by centuries the theorists who set down the notion of the state as an entity having an objective existence by itself, over and above its constituency.

The authority conferred by God upon the hierarchy and the ecclesiastical bodies was not shared by the other members of the Church. Here again the Christian unity was split into two sections, the *ecclesia docens* and the *ecclesia discens*—the clergy, the teachers and dispensers of grace, and the laymen, humble pupils who were to be instructed and guided. Between these two classes the gap became wider and wider when education and learning came to be almost the exclusive possession of the clergy and the word "layman" became a synonym for "rustic" and "illiterate." And since such histories as were written in those times were all the works of clerics, their outlook did not go beyond the sphere of ecclesiastical interests, privileges, rights and possessions, while the laity was looked upon as an inferior caste lacking all capacity to think or judge by themselves, to be led blindly, and above all to be distrusted and kept in submission by the fear of excommunications and interdicts, and by the fear of torture and death.

Another distinction was also introduced between the ecclesiastical office through which the Church performed its spiritual, moral, and soteric activities and the human personality of him who filled that office. The office as an emanation and manifestation of the Holy Spirit was sacred in itself and by itself, while the individual who held it, his character, his intelligence or ability, or sincerity of purpose were merely incidental things which did not affect the office and the authority which belonged to the office. In the theological and juridical doctrine of the sacraments, the validity and the efficiency of a sacramental performance is not dependent upon the moral character of the minister, even if he were the worst criminal imaginable. Just so, in the theology of history the value and the interpretation of historical events has little or no reference to individual factors as playing any considerable part in the final results. These are determined, not by human efforts or human weakness and faults, but by the divine will, which knows how to bring forth good out of evil, strength out of weakness, truth out of error, for the glorification and triumph of the Church!

But it was the myth of the chosen people in the form appropriated by the Church that played perhaps the most extensive role in shaping the features of the theology of history. The principle that the Church is the only agency entrusted directly by God with the unique and exclusive mission of procuring salvation, which is the supreme and final end of men, of society and its institutions, is very far-reaching in its implications. I can mention only the most obvious among them.

First of all, the Church as the instrument chosen to fulfill a divine mission has the right to possess all the means which are indispensable to perform its task. That is to say, the Church has by divine right all those powers which are essential to the functioning of authority in a well-ordered society: the power of legislation, the judiciary power, and the power of coercion. In other words, in the language of the jurists, the Church is a "*societas perfecta*" entitled to enact laws, to judge, absolve, or condemn and to apply its decisions by force if necessary. Since the same powers belong also to the state, which also is by definition a *societas perfecta*, the conflict of jurisdiction between Church and state must be eliminated not so much by a division of spheres of action, which in practice is impossible and has never been successful, as by the recognition of the highest claims of the Church, of its spiritual and universal character, as against the particularism and temporal character of the state; or, in a word, by the recognition of the universal direct or indirect jurisdiction of the Church over all phases and aspects of human individual and social life. A necessary consequence of this recognition is the principle of intolerance and coercion against all opposition to the powers of the Church. Truth and error, God and Satan, cannot be put on the same level and enjoy the same freedom. Error cannot be let loose to hamper the work of divine grace. Liberty of conscience and liberty of expression are liberties granted to Satan against the laws of God.

Looking back upon history from this point of view, institutional Christianity—the Church—appears in perspective as an essentially political entity in which religious, institutional, and temporal interests are all identified under the general classification of spiritual interests. And it is precisely upon this identification that the whole theological method of Christian historiography hinges. All opposition to the claims of the Church, whether doctrinal, coming from philosophy and science, or ethical, coming from mystical radicalism or spiritual simplicity, or practical, coming from the state and new political institutes, are all considered the product of diabolic pride of mind, *superbia mentis*, and of moral corruption, *corruptio cordis*. The rise of new ideas and the disappearance of old ones, political and social changes, conflicts and compromises, all the complex factors and the underlying forces of historical evolution are described and classified according to their relation to and their bearing upon the eternal, unchangeable, and divinely ordained *jura ecclesiae*, the rights of the Church, which take precedence over everything else.

The historiography of the Reformation remained essentially attached to the theological method. But having denied most of the claims of the institutional Church and having shifted the notion of authority from organized ecclesiasticism to the written revelation of the Bible, Protestant historians, beginning with the Centuriators of Magdeburg, rewrote the history of the Church with the purpose of finding in it the historical demonstration of their new theological position. This challenge had to be met by the Catholic side, and thus, as a by-product of the theological controversy, a reexamination of the evidence concerning the origin and growth of Christianity became a polemical necessity. On the other hand, the shifting of the weight of authority to the Bible led inevitably to a new scrutiny of the sacred texts, raising controversies about authenticity and textual tradition. Meanwhile, the humanistic revival of learning and the culture of the Renaissance had begun to provide new instruments of critical analysis of texts by the philological method.

The critical and textual method applied to the Old and the New Testaments led to a radical revision of all the traditional theories concerning not only the Biblical texts as literary works but also the history of Israel and of Judaism, as well as the history of Christian origins. Last but not least, the critical analysis of Biblical literature forced upon theology radical changes in the notion of inspiration and revelation.

In the wake of the Renaissance came the downfall of scholasticism and the rise of modern philosophy, together with scientific progress by the experimental method, which gradually changed the whole intellectual outlook on the world of nature and, as a consequence, on the world of the spirit. Still more devastating for the theological method of history was the rise of the *history of religions*. From the end of the eighteenth and throughout the nineteenth century, the advance in philological, anthropological, and archeological sciences made possible great progress in the study of primitive as well as historical religions. This development was soon followed by the *comparative history of religions*: the attempt to classify the great variety of religious forms and phenomena which constitute such an important part of universal history. The abundant material available from so many periods and sources suggested a new approach through the *psychology of religion*, aiming at the illustration of the inner processes, from the most elementary and instinctive to the highest and most complex forms of religious experience. Last but not least, the *philosophy of religion* began the task of making a synthesis of all the rational, sub-rational, and supra-rational elements of thought and of experience which form the substance of religion.

Christian historiography was affected in two ways by this development. First of all, in dealing with the history of non-Christian religions western scholars had no theological bias and had no apologetic purpose. Unlike a devoted Mohammedan historian, who believed in the reality of Mohammed's conversations with angels and in the heavenly character of the Koran, the lay historian of Islam could find a satisfactory explanation of those phenomena in Mohammed's psychology, in the circumstances of time and place, and in the environment in which Mohammed lived and thought. But, if it was satisfactory and legitimate to deal with those religions by such a method—and no other method would have been justified—why then should an exception be made in dealing with the history of Christianity?

Still more important in its implications was the fact that the detailed knowledge of various religions and their comparisons with Christianity revealed not only striking parallelisms in the process of formation and development of religions, but also close similarities in many a point of doctrine or of ritual. Above all, the reconstruction of the history of the Hellenistic religious world provided for the first time the right historical background needed for the understanding of the historical process of Christian origins. Religious notions and ideas which were once thought to be the exclusive and original contributions of Christianity alone, appeared to be the result of evolution of preexisting elements. The historian of Christianity no longer found it possible to isolate his subject, and to deal with it as with something which was unique and had in itself alone the reason for its existence, its growth, and its inner vitality.

We have thus traced a bare outline of the successive

stages of the theology of history and of the four structural myths on which it stands. As we have seen, these myths were not of Christian origin, but we must not overlook the important fact that these myths when adopted by Christianity, though preserving their outward mythological features, were at the same time penetrated by a new life-giving element of moral and spiritual ideas. The greatness of Christianity and its supreme importance in the history of mankind consisted precisely in having shifted the notion of the essential value of religion from ceremonial performances and legalistic equations to absolute moral requirements and lofty spiritual purposes.

Behind the mythological structure there was a high spiritual message which expressed what we may call the divinization of moral law as the supreme law of life of both God and man. Revelation in genuine spiritual Christianity had nothing to do with metaphysics or with intellectual casuistry; it consisted in the recognition that love of God and love of man are the sources of all moral behavior for the human individual and for human society. Under the awkward myth of the fall of man and of redemption there was the recognition that in altruism and self-sacrifice there is salvation and redemption from the evil and sordid aspects of life. The myth of the divine origin of authority enshrined in a divine setting the fundamental principle that a moral will holds the balance of human destiny; and finally the myth of the chosen race was but the expression of the vital principle that in a society based on moral will, moral values are the only standard for distinction and leadership.

At the beginning of the fourth century, the Christian apologist Lactantius described the bliss that the adoption of the Christian religion by the whole world would bring about: "If the true Christian God alone were worshipped, there would be no longer dissensions and wars. Men would all be united by undying love, for they would consider each other as brethren. Everyone would be satisfied with little; there would be no wars, no robberies, no graft. How happy would the condition of men be! What a golden age would begin for the world!"

Alas! For twenty centuries the Christian God has been worshipped in Europe but the golden age so naively foreseen by the Christian apologist has never been realized. After twenty centuries of Christianity we are witnessing today an explosion of ruthless barbarism unparalleled in history. And when we ask why we are engulfed in such a tempest of horrors, the teachers and guides of the Christian Church—popes, bishops, ministers and preachers—tell us that we are so afflicted because we have cast away God, the Christian God, from society and our life and have turned to worship the idols of power and lust and sin. Let us bring back God in our midst and we shall be saved. Was not this the language of the pagans when Rome was crumbling under the impact of the barbarians and of its own internal forces of disintegration? But was not the task of the Christian Churches and the only reason for their existence precisely that of keeping God in the individual and social life of mankind? Why has the Christian Church failed in its mission?

The historian can explain this failure only by the fact that the Churches, in their historical development, found it more convenient and useful to their institutional interests to stress the external structure of the old myths rather than the moral and spiritual content by which they had been reinterpreted in the original Christian message. The spirit was sacrificed to the letter, the spiritual freedom to the fetters of legalism, the mystic and moral elevation to the external social and economic advantages, the truly religious values to the political interests of the organization.

To be sure, theoretical and lip-service was always paid to moral values and spiritual purposes, but the Church, having become a political body, instead of furthering the process of spiritualization of the old myths in which they should have lost all their magical, material and political connotations, developed still more extensively their external mythological structure and became a prisoner of them, thus nullifying the vitality of the moral values of the original religious and social message of Christianity.

New currents of thought and new movements which finally assumed a definite and concrete form in the nineteenth century undertook the great task of demolishing the four old myths and of superseding them with new fundamental ideas which claimed the right to provide a better and more rational interpretation of human life and human history. These new ideas and notions themselves assumed, as was inevitable, the form of new myths to take the place of those to be discarded. And thus the myth of a divine revelation as an historical event, which took place in time and space and which enabled some men or some institutions to claim that they spoke with the voice of God, was superseded by the myth of science and philosophy in their broadest sense as being self-sufficient expressions of our intellectual life. The myth of the fall of mankind and of a mythological redemption was displaced by the myth of the indefinite progress of mankind through the growth of knowledge and the ripening of moral conscience. The myth of the divine authority of kings, governments or privileged groups, made room for the myth of popular sovereignty and of its concrete form, modern democracy. And last, the myth of the chosen race, either in a national and political sense or applied to an institutional religious body as being divine agents, was superseded by the myth of internationalism and of radical economic and social programs which should realize in practical and tangible form the great principle of the brotherhood of men.

The Christian Churches, and especially the great historical churches, denounced and condemned these new myths as being destructive not only of Christianity but of all religions. The denial of the special revelations which Churches and other religious bodies claim to possess was denounced as implying the denial of all supernatural life and of God himself. The confidence in the indefinite progress of mankind was pictured as a rebellion against the laws of God. Modern democracy was rejected because its fundamental principle of freedom of conscience was insulting the true and only God. Last but not least, the radical economic and social programs were anathematized as subversive of the order established by God and inimical to the rights of the Church.

The struggle between the old and the new myths was progressing to a decisive stage after the First World War. It was seen that there was urgent need for providing a new basis for the political, social and economic life of modern society, and the new forces at work, among hesitations and contradictions, outbursts of violence and timid recriminations, willful mistakes and chaotic new experiments, were constantly though slowly gaining ground. It was then that from the darkest corners of reaction a new gospel emerged, the gospel of Fascism and Nazism.

Fascism and Nazism claimed to be new and original philosophies of life, universal in content and scope and the logical result of the only true, realistic interpretation of human history. In fact, however, they were essentially new reincarnations of the four old myths, revived in their pre-Christian form and shorn of all those moral and spiritual values which Christianity had injected into them, at least in its teaching if not in its institutions.

As a matter of fact, Fascism and Nazism claim to be new revelations having the right to demand of their followers blind faith and blind obedience to their self-appointed and inspired leaders. As in the Christian revelation the instrument of God was the Church, universal, infallible and all-absorbing, so in the new revelation the instrument of God is the State, supreme and infallible master of all wills, of all powers, and of all resources. Both Fascism and Nazism have a dogmatic content based on the notion that mankind is organically corrupt and that human society organized on the recognition of individual rights and freedom under law is incapable of achieving any political and social order. Mankind needs new redeemers to slay the dragon of freedom and to secure salvation in slavery, massacres and wars of conquest.

Both Fascism and Nazism claim authority by a kind of divine right: the Duce, who can do no wrong, or the Fuehrer, who declares war and leads his armies by a kind of inspiration or intuition, do not hesitate to invoke the name of God as the source from which their power derives. Last but not least, the myth of the chosen race is set by them at the basis of the so-called new order which they claim will bring to fulfillment the plans of their God in human history. Strange as it may seem, Church leaders and all the sanctimonious conservatives in politics and economics thought at first that they had found in Fascism and Nazism a God-sent ally to curb for them the forces of freedom and of social and economic revolutions. In their blind confidence that the Fascist and Nazi reactions would stop at the door of religious principles and institutions and would protect all the vested temporal interests of the churches and the high classes of society, they rushed to shake hands with the "man of Providence" of Rome, and with the "crusader against Bolshevism" of Berlin.

They hastened to conclude with Fascism and Nazism concordats and agreements and then celebrated with thanksgivings the new era of peace, glory, and new advantages for the Church.

The identity of the myths which were behind the totalitarian systems with those which supplied the foundations of the Christian theology of history, was at least in part responsible for the fact that those churches failed to see that in the Fascist and Nazi savage new theology of history, there was no longer any room for moral principles or spiritual elements, and hence that churches and religions were also condemned to be destroyed by the triumph of totalitarianism. Only too late they began to realize their tragic error. But the same conservative and powerful churches have not yet realized, and perhaps it is impossible for them to realize, that their sweeping condemnation of the ideas and principles which have given rise to the new myths of freedom, of modern democracy, of progress and of radical social changes, is a no less tragic error than their initial confidence in the reactionary forces of Fascism.

There is no reason why a new political, social and economic order based on the new myths ought to be destructive of or inconsistent with religion. Only those who in hopeless confusion identify religion with ecclesiastical institutions, churches and groups which may have a religious name and a religious program, but are in fact political, social and economic groups, see in the new principles of our civilization a menace for religion.

There is no reason why science and philosophy, why a progressive social and economic order striving to reach a higher level, ought not to feel the need and to appreciate the value of a spiritual religion and of the spiritual worship of God, the sum total of all perfection and of goodness and of truth. In the humility of the true scientist who is fully aware of the limitations of his knowledge and who does not dare to affirm as true anything for which he has no sufficient evidence, there is more religion and more respect of God's will than in the pride and self-assurance of the theologian who speaks dogmatically of things that neither himself nor any other profess to understand. There is more true religious vision in the man who respects without reservations his brother's freedom to worship God in his own way according to his religious convictions, than in the intolerant churchman who justifies coercion and consigns to eternal perdition all those who do not share his beliefs. There is more intense religious life in the heart of the man who advocates an economic order that should fully realize the original Christian ideal of the brotherhood of men, than in the ranks of those who, to defend and to perpetuate temporal interests and privileges, are always ready to use the weapons of spiritual and moral pressure upon their followers and still more do not hesitate to provoke dissension and rebellions.

Theology of history proudly claims to know and to possess the monopoly of the plans of God for the world and has enshrined those plans in the un-Christian sanctuary of the old myths. The religious historian of today does not claim such a knowledge. But if history has a meaning for him, he can see in all humility God's will dimly reflected in the never ending struggle of mankind to conquer by its own efforts and deeds, through its own mistakes and crimes, that degree of spiritual and material freedom which is implied in the fundamental notions of the brotherhood of men and the fatherhood of God.